The Art of the Victorian Stage

By permission of Warwick Brookes, Manchester.

SIR HENRY IRVING.

The Art of the Victorian Stage

Notes and Recollections

BY

ALFRED DARBYSHIRE

BENJAMIN BLOM  New York/London

First Published 1907
Reissued 1969 by
Benjamin Blom, Inc., Bronx, New York 10452
and 56 Doughty Street, London, W.C. 1

Library of Congress Catalog Card Number 76-91898

Printed in U.S.A. by
NOBLE OFFSET PRINTERS, INC.
NEW YORK 3, N. Y.

To the memory of those dear Friends

Sir Henry Irving

and

Charles Alexander Calvert

whose work was honourable, and contributed

to the artistic value of the Victorian Stage,

I dedicate these

Notes and Recollections.

Alfred Darbyshire.

PREFACE.

I have undertaken the writing of this book at the earnest solicitation of friends, both on and off the stage. It is a record of my own experiences of stagecraft and stage art, during the last half century. This period of time embraces changes and fluctuations of great and important interest in the history of the English Stage. What I have attempted must be looked upon as a modest effort to record personal experiences in connection with the stage; and not in the light of a history. Many lives of actors and actresses have been written. These lives constitute a history of the English Stage from the Elizabethan, to the close of the Victorian epoch. In my Notes and Recollections I deal with that part of our national stage history in which I have had personal experiences.

I must tender my sincere thanks to those who have assisted me with statistical facts in connection with stage productions. I am especially indebted to my dear friend, the late Sir Henry Irving, Mr. Beerbohm Tree, Frank R. Benson, Mr. Robert Courtneidge and R. Flanagan, for information as to the plays produced under their management and the public appreciation as guaged by the number of performances.

I have introduced a few quotations from my book of "Experiences," contributions to journalistic literature, and from my address at the Arts Club, Manchester, on the 329th anniversary of the birth of Shakespeare.

I trust that nothing I have written will hurt or offend the feelings of the men and women whose art I have treated of, and I commend my humble effort to the kind consideration of the profession and to all lovers of the art of the Theatre.

A. D.

MANOR PARK,
KNUTSFORD, CHESHIRE, 1907.

CONTENTS.

———

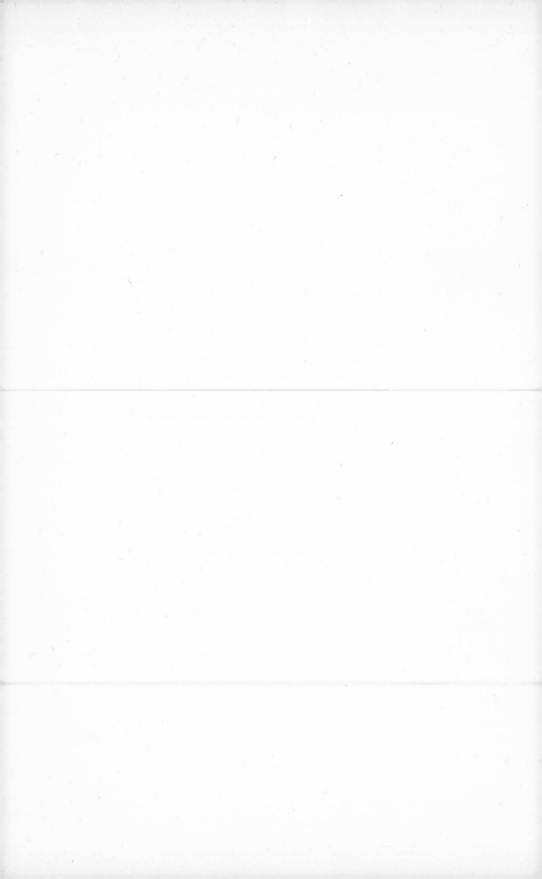

CHAPTER I.

THE ART OF THE STAGE.

IT is a curious and interesting fact that the two great periods of English histrionic art, are marked by the reigns of two great queens. The age of Elizabeth produced the greatest dramatist the world has ever known ; and the age of Victoria has given the greatest value to his works by stage illustration. It is a source of pride and high satisfaction that the immortal works of Shakespeare have in our own time been given to the world on the English stage free of academic conventionality, and with the result that their author dreamed of and hoped for when he wrote them.

Although the Elizabethan era will ever be held in respect and reverence as having given birth to the world's greatest dramatist, the Victorian era will also be respected and honoured in historic annals for having given truthful and beautiful stage expression to the Shakespearian creations.

Although honour was done to Shakespeare by the cultured people of Queen Elizabeth's reign, it is to Queen Victoria (almost from the moment she ascended the throne) we owe the fact that the stage of the nineteenth century became the medium of the *true* and beautiful method of expression of the Shakespearean drama.   Queen Victoria instituted the Windsor Theatricals, superintended by Charles Kean; and for years afterwards patronized the theatre when Shakespeare was given to the public through the medium of the stage.

It is interesting to review the history of the exposition of the drama comprised in the period of three hundred years, between the reigns of England's two great queens.   This, however, would require a volume different in scheme and object from this modest effort of "Recollections."   In order, however, to substantiate what I may hereafter say on the art of the Victorian stage, it is necessary to summarise the history of histrionic art from the time it was exhibited in the theatres of the Elizabethan period to its representation on the stage of the Victorian era.

When we contemplate the adverse conditions under which Shakespeare wrote and produced his plays for the Blackfriars playhouse and the Globe on the Bank Side, we should, I think, congratulate ourselves that we live in an age in which it is possible to do full justice to his works; and that although the reign of the great Elizabeth can boast the production of our Poet's genius, the reign of another great queen has produced the men whose high intellectual qualities have helped to enshrine that genius in the hearts of the English people by making it understood and appreciated through the art of the Victorian stage.

It should be borne in mind that the strange history and vicissitudes of dramatic art, in the period I am writing of, were owing to the political and religious troubles which followed the reign of James I., when actors fought for their king and died on the battlefield. Stage art underwent a change with the Stuart restoration in 1660, when clever writers prepared a certain kind of play suited to the frivolous life consequent on the severity of the Puritan administration and the closing of theatres in the reign of Charles I. Through all this history, adverse to the honour and welfare of the art of the stage, Shakespeare was almost forgotten ; and from the time of Betterton, to the latter half of the Georgian era, Shakespeare was little honoured by his countrymen.

The revival, which took place about the middle of the eighteenth century, found its complete expression in the acting of David Garrick. An academic and conventional school was established (although it is recorded that Garrick could act *naturally*) which became intensified through the Kemble period, and in the art of Cooke, Young, Edmund Kean and Macready. This form of histrionic art lingered until the end of Barry Sullivan's career. Sullivan's art was the echo of what has been called the "high and palmy" school of acting ; but we who saw it are enabled, by contrast with the modern Victorian school, to arrive at a fair conclusion as to the proper method of expressing the great Shakespearian drama.

It will naturally be asked, what is the proper method

of stage representation ?   Before such a question can be
answered it is necessary to arrive at a conclusion as to
what is comprehended in the term *histrionic art ?*   Is
it the art of *acting* only, or does it include the complete
art of stage representation ?   In considering such a
question it is necessary to deal with what I still fear is
a *vexato quæstio* with some persons.   Did Shakespeare
write to be *read* or to be *acted ?*   Because on this issue
depends the whole question of stage representation.

It seems almost an idle waste of time to discuss this
point; but as there are still some few students and scholars
who cling to the old-fashioned idea, that our Poet's
works should only be recited or declaimed from a
platform with a green baize screen behind the persons
so reciting or declaiming, it is necessary to give the
matter some consideration.

I consider that the term *histrionic art* means the
combination of vocal expression and bodily action, with
such adjuncts and surroundings as it is possible for the
stage to supply.   To achieve this result has been the
aim and high ambition of those responsible for the art
of the Victorian stage.

On this question of stage representation it is curious
that amongst the advocates of this combination are to
be found the names of celebrated ecclesiastics, men of
culture and high intellectuality; such, for instance, as
the late great and good James Fraser, Lord Bishop of
Manchester, and His Eminence Cardinal Wiseman.
It may not be generally known that Cardinal Wiseman
devoted some of the last hours of his life to recording

his thoughts upon our great Poet and his works. His last literary effort was to dictate during an illness his lecture on William Shakespeare. After saying that he had never in his life seen Shakespeare acted he goes on to say that this was to his disadvantage, for Shakespeare wrote *to be acted* and *not to be read*. After a declaration like this what more need be said? Yet mark how strong within him was the scholar's enthusiasm. He says:—

"But on the other hand, is it not something to have approached this wonderful man, and to have communed with him in silence and in solitude, face to face with him alone ; to have read, and studied, and meditated on him in early youth, without gloss or commentary or preface or glossary? For such was my good or evil fortune ; not during the still hours of night, but during that stiller portion of an Italian afternoon, when silence is deeper than in the night, under a bright and sultry sun when all are at rest, all around you hushed to the very footsteps in a well-peopled house, except the unquelled murmuring of a fountain beneath orange trees, which mingled thus the most delicate of fragrance with the most soothing of sounds, both stealing together through the half-closed windows of wide and lofty corridors."

Yet after all this ecstacy His Eminence could frankly declare that "Shakespeare wrote to be acted, and not to be read."

As Shakespeare wrote for the stage, and not for the scholar, how should the stage give expression to his inspired works? On this point, I have only one opinion. All that art, intellect, and stagecraft can produce, should be forthcoming to provide a glorious setting suitable for the brightest jewels which have ever sparkled from the human brain. I am conscious that in writing thus strongly I shall come into contact with those persons who are content with a *moderate* setting of the Shakespearian drama, and who joined in the cry against Charles Kean, when he was called the "Upholsterer," and not the upholder of the drama. It has always seemed to me a strange thing that this class of objectors, to complete representation, should not have taken the trouble to look into the Poet's own pages for some argument in favour of their theory. Perhaps they have done so, and found all the internal evidence against them ; at least such I judge to be the case, inasmuch as I have failed to detect, as yet, any authoritative utterance on the subject ; and one would fain believe that the often ill-natured and ignorant criticism of a quarter of a century ago has disappeared, and died a natural death in face of the superb conditions under which we now behold the Shakespearian drama.

I have often thought, whilst helping in a small way to do honour to the memory of Shakespeare by worthy representation of his works, that if the spirits of the departed know ought of this world which held them in the flesh, then the great spirit of our Poet, as it moves through the "Elysian Fields," will look with satisfaction and approval on what has been done, and what is still being done, to honour his memory. Let us remember how that spirit cried out after the creation of the historical play of " Henry the Fifth."

" O for a muse of fire, that would ascend
  The brightest heaven of invention,
  A Kingdom for a stage, princes to act
  And monarchs to behold the swelling scene ! "

And again :—

" But pardon gentles all
  The flat unraised spirits that have dared
  On this unworthy scaffold to bring forth
  So great an object ; can this cockpit hold
  The vasty fields of France ? or, may we cram
  Within this wooden O the very casques
  That did affright the air at Agincourt."

    .   .   .   .   .   .

" Pierce-out our imperfections with your thoughts ;
  Into a thousand parts divide one man,
  And make imaginary puissance ;
  Think, when we talk of horses, that you see them
  Printing their proud hoofs i' the receiving earth ;
  For 'tis your thoughts that now must deck our kings."

All this shows how keenly Shakespeare felt the inadequacy of his tome to give expression to the pictures that filled his fertile brain; for although the first four collected editions of his works (the last dated 1685) do not give a "local habitation and a name" to the scenes of his dramas, we cannot doubt for a moment but that these scenes arose vividly before his imagination.   The First Folio describes the action of "The Tempest" as taking place in an uninhabited island, but it would be an insult to the genius of the great poet of nature to suppose when creating that beautiful work that "his eye in a fine frenzy rolling" did not see the sylvan scenes of that "Enchanted

Island," as Pope calls it.   Yes, assuredly he would see that fearful tempest; he would hear the sailors cry out amidst its howling and hissing; then the beautiful calm; the sunlight flitting across the hills, darting down the dales into the woods and over the purling brooks and far away across the blue depth of the Mediterranean Sea.   He would hear that strange music which filled the isle, and he would follow the flight of his dainty Ariel as he shaped out the lives and destinies of the foolish mortals who make up the human interest of these enchanting scenes.

In the autumn of 1902, Sir Henry Irving was in Manchester at the Theatre Royal.   I accompanied him to a morning performance, at the Prince's Theatre, of "As You Like It," the last revival by Robert Courtneidge, the cultured and enthusiastic manager of the theatre.   On the final fall of the curtain we quietly rose, and Irving offered no remark on what he had seen.   I looked at him, and said, "Well! is the effort a good one, will it do?"   He looked at me with a quiet, happy smile, and said, "Well, my boy, I have seen exactly what Shakespeare saw as he wrote the immortal comedy.   I am thankful."   This was a corroboration, by a great actor, of the truth of the theory I have propounded in writing of "The Tempest."   At a luncheon given to Sir Henry Irving by the Lord Mayor of Manchester, he spoke in the highest terms of praise of the revival by Mr. Courtneidge, and the consequence was, that thousands of playgoers from all parts of the country crowded the little, historic Prince's

Theatre, to see "As You Like It" as Shakespeare saw it when he wrote the words as coming from the mouths of those who lived and moved amid the sylvan shades and under the "melancholy boughs" of the Forest of Arden.

In working out the loveliest comedy ever written Shakespeare would, in "As You Like It," live in the scenes of his dramatic action; he would plunge into the depths of the forest; he would pause in some opening glade and gaze on the refined beauty of "Heavenly Rosalind" as she leans against some huge forest monarch conning those love tales woman delights in. He would see in an opening gorge the gentle deer come tripping out of the pine forest and cross

> "The current that with gentle murmur glides
> And makes sweet music with the enamell'd stones."

Suddenly he would see the herd startled and dart into the opposite wood, leaving the languishing one that

> "From the hunter's aim had ta'en a hurt"

augmenting the swift brook with tears.

When working out the beauties of his plays, purely imaginative in idea and scene, his mind was free and unshackled; the scenes were simply nature; but in dealing with events of history Shakespeare's mind pictured the scenes in which the action took place. The quotation I have given from the Chorus in "Henry V" clearly indicates that in rolling out that blank verse he pictured the actual scenes; he followed the progress of the French campaign, he saw that glorious battle, the triumphal entry into London, and the magnificent nuptials of his favourite hero and the fair Catherine of France. Again—in "Julius Cæsar"—his poetic fancy would hurry him along till he saw that Hall of a Hundred Columns, built by Pompeius Magnus in the Plains of the Campus Martius; he would follow the conspirators with the noble Brutus at their head as they hurried up the slopes of the Capitol brandishing their weapons, red with the blood of the greatest man on earth.

And so on through the entire range of his Histories, Tragedies and Comedies, his great mind dwelt on actual scenes, whether historic or ideal, and as a play-wright, actor, and manager, he would naturally regret the want of resource of the stage of his time, and indulge in the hope of better days to come. How vainly he cherished this hope. The first effort made to develop the resources of the theatre resulted in disaster. When "Henry VIII." was produced the wads from the *real* cannon let off at the christening of the infant princess, lodged in the thatched roof of the Globe Theatre and removed that "Cockpit," that "Wooden O," from the face of the earth.

Bearing these considerations and facts in mind, can we be surprised that enthusiastic devotees exist who have taken advantage of the resources of the nineteenth century to worthily and adequately produce his works? Is it to be wondered at that the great actor-managers, Kean, Phelps, Calvert, Tree, Courtneidge, Benson, and Irving, have spent the best years of their lives, and their treasure, in efforts to place Shakespeare upon our stage with all the accessories and surroundings calculated to secure an honourable setting for the jewels of his mind? Surely we cannot but approve of these noble efforts; let us then welcome them as a fitting tribute of respect and adoration which the resources of our age have enabled us to bestow on the genius of William Shakespeare.

Charles Kean was the pioneer in this great movement; his efforts, therefore, demand primary attention and consideration. I had the good fortune to witness his production of "Henry VIII." at the Princess's Theatre, and, although I was deeply impressed by it, I am astonished when I review the progress made, and at the development of the resources of the theatre since that time. It must be borne in mind that, with the exception of that rendered by the venerable Planché *(Somerset Herald)* and George Scharf, F.S.A., Charles Kean had little outside assistance in his work. Sir Henry Irving commanded the best energies of a Tadema, a Lucas, or a "Garter King;" men of art and literature have been proud of association with our great actor-manager in his work; and the highest antiquarian and artistic knowledge was at his disposal.

When I review the work of Charles Kean, I am impressed with its magnitude and importance. If the world owes a debt of gratitude to Hemming and Condell for the preservation of Shakespeare's work, to Charles Kean belongs the credit of producing that work on the stage, in a manner calculated to display its beauty and its sublimity before the English people.

CHAPTER II.

CHARLES KEAN.

CHARLES KEAN opened the Princess's Theatre, in Oxford Street, London, in September, 1850. I shall confine my notes on Charles Kean to a brief record of his work of producing the Shakespearian drama from what may be called the "Revival" standpoint. In other words, a method of production which the English stage had never seen, and in which the men and women lived and moved in the scenery and localities of their lifetimes, and in the costumes wherewith they were clothed. It is difficult to do justice to this great work of Kean's, as I have only witnessed one of his revivals, "Henry VIII." After seeing one of the productions at the Princess's, under Kean's management, it is difficult to realise the disadvantageous conditions under which the Shakespearian drama had been given to the English play-going public anterior to the middle of the nineteenth century. Killigrew and Davenent inaugurated a great reform by having women to act women's parts, hitherto played by boys and youths. Sir William Davenent also made a modest effort at scenic mounting, but "Macbeth" continued to be played in Georgian costume until varied by the Kembles, Macready, and Edmund Kean. Looking at the picture, by Zoffany, of Garrick and Mr. Pritchard in their great scene in "Macbeth" (still hanging on the walls of the Garrick Club) it seems a strange thing that the great Scottish king and his wife should be dressed in lace coat, ruffles, tights, powdered wigs and robes of the court of George III. Yet this is the sort of thing our ancestors had to be contented with till the Victorian era abolished such anachronisms under the revolutionary action of Charles Kean.

On opening the Princess's Theatre, Charles Kean presented "Twelfth Night" and "Hamlet." These were not strictly "Revivals," but in the following year, the great idea of his life dawned upon him, and then followed that series of splendid productions with which his name will ever be associated. The "Merchant of Venice" was produced in 1851, succeeded by "Merry Wives of Windsor," "King John," "Much Ado about Nothing," "Macbeth," "Richard III.," "Henry IV.," "Winter's Tale," "Midsummer Night's Dream," Richard II.," "The Tempest," "King Lear," and "Henry V." I shall hereafter allude to the production of the last play by Charles Calvert, but it is a curious thing that the art of the stage, in 1859 and in 1872, reached its culminating point in the representation of the life and heroism of the Victor of Agincourt. Charles Kean spent his best energies, and gave expression to his profound knowledge of Mediæval times in the production of " Henry V."; the same may be truly said of the effort in the same direction made by Charles Calvert at the little Prince's Theatre in the City of Manchester.

I have gathered from reliable sources of information, that Charles Kean first attempted the realisation of his ideas of mounting the Shakespearian drama when he produced " King John," in February of 1852. Of this event, I note that J. W. Cole, in his "Life and Theatrical Times of Charles Kean, F.S.A," says :—

"No longer fettered by restraining influences, and confident in the result although previous experiments were attended by failure, he entered boldly on the enterprise. The result is before the public. It has worked a total revolution in the dramatic system by the establishment of new theories and the subversion of old ones. The time had at length arrived when a total purification of Shakespeare, with every accompanyment that refined knowledge, diligent research, and chronological accuracy could supply, was suited to the taste and temper of the age, which had become eminently pictorial and exacting beyond all former precedent. The days had long passed when audiences could believe themselves transported from Italy to Athens by the power of poetical enchantment without the aid of scenic appliances."

In 1853, Kean produced " Macbeth," which was first performed before the Queen at Windsor Castle. A "Fly Leaf" was attached to the ordinary play bill, in which, reasons were given for the method of mounting the work and the authorities quoted for the architecture, costumes and armour displayed. This explanation created a sensation, and, in addition, a book was printed as a record of its production. This idea of a printed edition of the Shakespeare plays, produced by Charles Kean. was maintained for "Henry VIII.," "Winter's Tale," "Midsummer Night's Dream," Richard II.," "The Tempest," "King Lear," "Merchant of Venice," "King John," "Much Ado about Nothing," "Hamlet," and "King Henry V."

On reviewing the work of Charles Kean, from the information at my disposal, I have concluded that the "Revivals" of "King John," "Macbeth," "Winter's Tale," and " Henry V." may be looked upon as masterpieces of knowledge, research, and art work. Of course, the work of other authors was well produced, especially the "Sardanapalus" of Lord Byron, and in which Kean was materially assisted by Layard, the discoverer of ancient Nineveh.

It was absolutely essential that the art of acting should keep pace with art of production; and consequently we find on the Princess's play-bills the names of some of the best actors and actresses of the Kean period, including Walter Lacy, Mr. Ryder, and young Ellen Terry. I had the pleasure of making the acquaintance of Miss Terry and Walter Lacy during my professional work in connection with the alterations and decorations at the Lyceum, when the late Sir Henry Irving went into possession at the end of 1878. Perhaps no actress of the latter half of the Victorian era has had such an influence for the good of the art of the theatre as Ellen Terry; but I must refrain from further allusion until I come to treat of Irving's great work at the Lyceum.

It was a day of regret when Charles Kean took leave of the Princess's Theatre on the 29th of August, 1859. A few extracts from his farewell speech may be of interest. The valedictory addresses of our "Revival" managers are full of interest and seem to explain or sum up the work of their lives.

At the close of the performance of "Henry VIII." Charles Kean said:—

"This night concludes my Managerial career. The good ship which I have commanded for nine years, through storm and sunshine, calm and tempest is now about to re-enter harbour, and in nautical phrase to be paid off. I may, perhaps, be expected on an occasion like the present to make some allusion to the principles of management I have invariably adopted. I have always entertained the conviction that in illustrating the great plays of the grandest poet who ever wrote, historical accuracy might be so blended with pictorial effect, that instruction and amusement would go hand in hand. *I find it impossible that because every detail is studied with an eye to truth, such a plan can in the most remote degree detract from the beauties of the Poet.*"

"I remember that when I produced the 'Winter's Tale' as a Greek play, that is with Greek dresses, Greek customs and Greek Architecture, an objection was raised by some, that although the scene was situated in Syracuse—then a Greek colony—whose King consults the celebrated Oracle of Delphi—yet the play was said to be essentially English, and ought to be so presented because allusions in various parts bore reference to this country, and to the period when the author wrote."

"You would, perhaps, have been somewhat astonished and perplexed, to have seen the chest containing the answer of the Greek Oracle to the Greek King, supposed to have been delivered above two thousand years ago, borne upon the stage by the Beefeaters of Queen Elizabeth. You would, perhaps, have been equally surprised to have witnessed at this Theatre, Leontes as a Greek King in the last Act, attired as Hamlet, Prince of Denmark, and yet such an incongruity was accepted within the last twenty years."

. . . . . .

"But to carry out my system of pictorial illustration, the cost has been enormous, far too great for the limited arena in which it was incurred. As a single proof I may state, that in this little Theatre where £200 is considered a large receipt, and £250 an extraordinary one, I expended in one season alone a sum little short of £50,000. During the run of some of the great revivals as they are called, I have given employment and consequently weekly payment to nearly 550 persons."

. . . . . .

"Having said thus much, I need not deny that I have been no gainer in a commercial sense. I do not now retire from the direction of this Theatre through any feeling of disappointment, but from the remembrance of the old adage, 'The pitcher goes often to the well, but the pitcher at last may be broken.'"

. . . . .

After alluding to his forthcoming Provincial tour, he concluded by saying :—

"Let me fondly cherish the hope that you will sometimes bestow a thought on the absent wanderer; and confiding in your sympathy and regard, I now respectfully and gratefully take my leave, bidding you 'Farewell—a long Farewell.'"

The present race of playgoers would more easily understand the value of Charles Kean's great work, if they could contrast it with the state of the art of the theatre at the commencement of the Victorian era. The changes and reforms he introduced have resulted in the removal of a prejudice in many circles of English life, and the theatre is now looked upon, by all classes of society, as a public institution of value in modern civilisation.

It has always been a source of satisfaction to myself that, in addition to the appreciation of the general public, the antiquarian knowledge and archæological research of Charles Kean were recognised by the Society of Antiquaries; and that he was elected a Fellow of that honourable institution. As Henry Irving was the first actor knighted by the reigning sovereign, so Charles Kean was the first, and I think the only actor ever honoured by being elected a Fellow of the Society of Antiquaries. These two honours I look upon as of much value to the art of the stage, and as practical evidence of respect to the profession from those by whom they were conferred.

My personal knowledge of Charles Kean was brief and sad. The great actor-manager came to Manchester in 1867. In the month of May he appeared with Mrs. Kean at the Theatre Royal. "King Richard II." was performed on Friday, the 10th, which performance I attended. In the same week "King John was performed, and I shall always remember that night. I was present with Mr. G. Vernon Marsh, then the scholarly dramatic critic of the *Manchester Guardian*. The play had not proceeded far when we became conscious that something was wrong, and the staggering and half fainting movements of Mr. Kean proved that illness had seized him. The play was concluded and Mr. Kean was removed to the Palatine Hotel, where he was staying with Mrs. Kean and his niece, Miss Chapman, who was a member of the theatrical company. Mr. Marsh and myself called to see Mr. Kean on the following morning, and we came to the conclusion that his acting days were nearly over. He died in the following year, 1868. His death took from the theatrical world a manager and actor who may be acknowledged as the pioneer of the reformation of the art of the Victorian stage.

CHAPTER III.

SAMUEL PHELPS.

I NEVER saw Macready, and have no "Notes or Recollections" of him.   Sir Frederick Pollock, Bart, one of his executors, has written a life of the great actor, from which may be obtained all information as to the important part he played in the art of the Victorian stage.

Although I had no personal knowledge of Macready, who died in 1873, I have some pleasant recollections of the man who assisted him in the delineation of the high class drama.   I refer to Samuel Phelps.   These two great actors may be called the reformers of the art of the stage, when vacated by Garrick and his talented, but conventional successors.

What shall I say of the life work of Samuel Phelps? I confess when I think of what he accomplished in the direction of an artistic representation of Shakespeare on our stage I experience feelings of astonishment and gratitude.   He fought the battle of Shakespearean production against fearful odds, and in the face of a prejudice begotten of a degraded taste.   I have called

Charles Kean the pioneer of what we are pleased to call " Revivals," but Phelps was certainly the originator of what we understand by the word *"Productions."* There is a difference in meaning between these two terms. In the first case the pieces are staged with that elaborate detail and accuracy resulting from scholarly and antiquarian knowledge under the control of the actor-manager; in the latter case the Shakespearean drama is exhibited in a beautiful and appropriate setting, which may be called the intermediate method between the slip-shod style of the Garrick era, and the method of production inaugurated by Kean, continued by Calvert, and brought to its utmost limit of completeness by Irving. Although the method adopted by Phelps was not as elaborate as that of the "Revivalists" its effect upon the Shakespearean stage of our time was wonderful, and this country may ever hold in high esteem the memory of Samuel Phelps for the noble efforts he made to bring the works of our Poet home to the hearts of the people, through his beautiful and appropriate *"Productions."* I sometimes think we are apt to forget, or at all events we fail to realise, the Titanic work of this great actor and manager. Think for a moment of the task he set himself to perform; and of what he actually accomplished for the art of the stage. He did not seek to labour in the heart of fashionable London; he sought out a suburban theatre attached to the old historic "Sadler's Wells," in Islington, planted the works of our immortal bard in rude, uncultivated soil, and for a period of nearly nineteen years he never ceased in his efforts to make that soil receptive of all that was beautiful and actable from the Shakespearean page.

In 1851 Charles Dickens wrote:—

"Seven or eight years ago this Theatre (Sadler's Wells) was in the condition of being entirely delivered over to as ruffianly an audience as London could shake together. Without, the Theatre by night was like the worst of the worst kind of Fair in the worst kind of town. Within, it was a bear-garden, resounding with foul language, oaths, cat-calls, shrieks, yells, blasphemy, obscenity, a truly diabolical clamour. Fights took place anywhere at any period of the perform-ance, and the audience were of course directly addressed in the entertainments."

. . . . . .

"Phelps conceived the desperate idea of changing the character of the dramatic entertainments presented at this den from the lowest to the highest, and of utterly changing with it the character of the audience."

. . . . . .

"It is to be observed," says Dickens, "that these plays have not been groaned through in the old jog-trot dreary, matter of course manner, but have been presented with the utmost care, with great intelligence, with an evidently sincere desire to understand and illustrate the beauties of the poem. The smallest character has been respectfully approached and studied; the smallest accessory has been well considered, every artist in his degree has been taught to adapt his part in the complete effect to all the other parts uniting to make up the whole."

. . . . . .

"A completeness has been attained which twenty times the cost would never have bought if Mr. Phelps were not a gentleman in spirit, and an accomplished and devoted student of his Art."

Phelps opened Sadler's Wells Theatre in conjunc-tion with Mrs. Warner in 1844 with "Macbeth," and he left the scene of his labours on the 6th November, 1862, in the character of Brutus. During this period, he produced no less than thirty-four plays of Shakespeare; in fact, all the First Folio Plays, with the exception of the three parts of "Henry VI.," "Troilus and Cressida," "Richard II.," and "Titus Andronicus." He also produced "Pericles," which did not appear in the compilation published by Hemming and Condell in 1623.

Truly this is a noble record. It was the work of a hero. Phelps was a genial, kind-hearted gentleman, a great actor, and a man of attainments consequent on a high intellectuality. Although he did not exhibit his knowledge to the full extent in his stage productions, he possessed the culture which would have enabled him to make those "productions" partake of the character of "Revivals," had he so desired. I remember on one of those occasions when he came to the old Brasenose Club in Manchester to rest and chat, I turned the conversation on Irving's forthcoming production of "Hamlet." At that time my antiquarian knowledge was not very profound, and I happened to tell Phelps that Irving was going to wear a scarlet cloak. "Quite right," was his reply. "Don't you know, my boy, that scarlet was the mourning colour of the royal house of Denmark at the period of the play?" "Ah!" he said, "Irving is a plucky man, I would not have dared to do that at Sadler's Wells."

I am thankful to say that I saw dear old Phelps act, although it was at an advanced age and in the decline

of his great powers, during the career of Charles
Calvert at the Prince's Theatre, in the City of Man-
chester, which marked a decade of the finest Shakespearean Revivals which have ever been known. Phelps
visited his old friend between closing the doors of
Sadler's Wells Theatre in 1862, after the work of
eighteen years, and his final engagement in London.
The grand old actor impersonated his immortal character of "Bottom the Weaver" in "A Midsummer
Night's Dream" : at different dates, he played for
Calvert, Malvolio in "Twelfth Night," and Falstaff in
"The Merry Wives of Windsor." It was, however,
in the production of "Henry IV." (second part) that
Phelps rose to the full height of his genius by doubling
the parts of the King and Justice Shallow. This event
took place in 1874, and became historic in theatrical
annals. I was present when this was arranged, and the
way it came about was curious and interesting.

When the old manager of Sadler's Wells entered
the Brasenose Club, Manchester, he was received with
tokens of respect and high regard. He invariably
seated himself between the arms in the centre of a long
ottoman, and around him would gather his fellow
members to listen to angling adventures and anecdotes
of stage life. I remember on one occasion he entered
with Calvert. "Business" was not quite what they
expected at the theatre, and Calvert said, " Let us put
up 'Sir Pertinax Macsycophant.'" Phelps replied, "No!
I am sick of every word he ever uttered." They
decided to put up "A Midsummer Night's Dream." The

whirligig of time is a strange thing; here was Charles
Calvert (now the prosperous actor-manager), who
confessed that he had learned his art, and fixed his
career, from seeing Phelps, talking to the old tragedian
on the business of the theatre. It was on this occasion,
that Calvert suggested to Phelps the production of
"Henry IV.," and that the latter should double the
parts of the King and Justice Shallow. The great
man calmly stroked his chin, and said, "A capital idea,
Calvert! we'll do it." The result of this conversation
was, as I have said, a matter of history in stage annals.
What may be called the "Old Double" scene was the
work of the highest dramatic art, and will never be
forgotten by those who saw it. "Old Double" is dead
and so is the last member of the old school of acting.
Lovers of the drama know his genial presence no more,
but on the roll of this country's dramatic history will
ever remain the name of Samuel Phelps. ·

*In the year 1877 Phelps took his final leave of
Manchester, and the good old Brasenose Club, of which
he was a member marked the event by presenting him
with an address, illuminated and appropriately bound.
I was one of the deputation who presented this address
at his lodgings, where he was staying with his daughter,
Miss Esther Phelps. I recollect he told us a story of
his first appearance in Manchester as a young man, at

---

* I remember that in connection with this production of "Henry IV."
I had my first sight and knowledge of young J. Forbes Robertson, who
played "Prince Harry"; he added materially to the *tout ensemble* of the
production; and it is pleasant to know that with riper years he became one
of the representative actors of the Victorian Stage, as an exponent of the
Shakespearean Drama.

the old Theatre Royal in Fountain Street. On this occasion the gas of the theatre, both on the stage and in the auditorium, became extinguished, and left the entire theatre in darkness. Being inclined to superstition he took this as a bad omen and looked upon his future as a probable failure. That this superstitious dread was a mistake the world knows well.

A copy of the address has been preserved, and although printed in "The Life and Life Work of Samuel Phelps," by W. May Phelps and J. Forbes Robertson, I insert it in these pages, with the names of men of local note and celebrity attached.

To
Samuel Phelps, Esq.,
from
The Brazennose Club,
Manchester.

Dear Sir,

A few of your fellow-members of the Brazennose Club desire in this form to bid you a respectful and affectionate adieu on your approaching retirement from the stage.

We only follow universal opinion in recognizing in you one of the last, and assuredly not the least, of those who, through the course of a lifetime devoted to the culture and exposition of the noble dramatic literature of the country, have laboured, whether as actor or manager, to consecrate the theatre to its highest purposes.

Were it your merited praise simply to have founded with your own hands an asylum for the disregarded and declining drama, and to have maintained it by your genius and perseverance with such success, that a remote and infrequented suburb of London became for years the centre of attraction to Shakespearean students, a school of reviving taste, and the rallying ground of lofty impulses not yet we would believe, exhausted, your name would deserve to be held in lasting recollection and esteem.

We also, however, honour in you the gifted personal expositor of numerous beautiful and instructive creations, endowed through you for thousands of hearers with a charm and intensity of meaning which without your powerful aid, they would never have been discovered to possess.

To one who has exerted himself with so much success to raise the national character by refining the intellectual amusements of the people, it is no exaggeration to address the language applied by the Poet Laureate to one of your most distinguished predecessors, Mr. Macready, on his taking leave of the profession in which he was intimately associated with yourself—

> " Rank with the best
> Garrick and statelier Kemble and the rest,
> Who made a nation purer through their Art
> Thine is it that our drama did not die
> Nor flicker down to brainless pantomime,
> And those gilt gauds men-children swarm to see."

We reflect with pleasure on the bond of union between you and this Club, which will not be broken by the cessation of your periodical visits to Manchester.

If our local opportunities of seeing you have been comparatively few, they have been all the more warmly cherished, and it is with sincere regret that, while hoping for you many years of deserved repose, in private life, we face the necessity of bidding you, in your public capacity, a grateful and admiring *Farewell*.

> Joseph Manchester, Chairman.
> L. W. Andrews, Treasurer.
> Jno. Robt. Newby, Hon. Secretary.

Brazennose Street, Manchester,
    March 17th, 1877.

Alfred Aspland, F.R.C.S.

T. Walton Gillibrand

William Alfred Turner

Arthur G. Symonds, M.A.

William Bright Morris

William Leader

Henry Measham

George Evans, F.R.S.L.

Charles Escourt, F.C.S.

Harry Bridson, M.A.

J. Lees Aspland, M.A.

Fra. Hampton

Samuel Taylor, M.A.

Richard Smith, B.A.

J. Fox Turner

Thomas C. Johnson

Charles Schuster

J. Edge Partington

G. W. Smith

F. R. B. Lindsell

John Nelson

E. Hulton

Alfred Darbyshire, F.I.B.A.

H. M. Brazil

Edward de Jong, Chevalier

John Slagg

Henry Watkinson

H. M. Acton

Samuel Beaumont

Alfred Sington

Frank Merriman

Edward G. Simpson

Thomas Swanston

William Grimshaw

F. A. Haserick

William Knight Keeling

F. P. Rickards

T. Edmondson

H. W. J. Tracie

J. J. Armitage

George Freemantle

H. E. Prest

Thomas Browning

George Falkner

John Bagshaw

W. D. Jeans

Abel Heywood, Junr.

William C. Lord

Joseph B. Forster

Thomas Worthington

Selim Rothwell

J. H. Davies

William Morton

William Hull

Wllliam Lamb Hockin

William Warburton

Robert Pollett

J. F. Faraday

J. Houghton Hague

J. Ewald Pendleton

E. Leader Williams, Junr.

Edward Milner

R. W. Edmondson

James H. Lynde

Gustav Voigt

Peter Allan

Henry Knowles, L.R.C.P.

Edward F. Lloyd, R.E.

Leonard Tatham

William Sidney

Robert Leake

J. H. E. Partington

Christopher Sparrow
John Angell, F.C.S.
Edwin Waugh
A. H. Danes Colley
Nath. Cartwright
John Dewhurst Milne
Henry A. Schwabe
Charles R. Allen
Howarth Ashton
T. C. d'Angiuer
W. R. R. Gemmell
George H. Fryer
John Shuttleworth
E. Solomons
Vernon Cochrane
J. G. Lynde

J. G. Wehner
James Lamb
Thomas Tatham
Ottley S. Perry
Richard Gay Somerset
H. Bowman
Christian Reimers
W. J. Buckley
Samuel Barlow
G. Sheffield
George Hayes
Edward T. Bellhouse
Edward Atkinson
William Abercrombie
John Heywood
Samuel Buckley, F.R.C.S.

Much has been said and written on Samuel Phelps and his work ; I have already quoted Charles Dickens on the subject, but I think I cannot conclude my notes and recollections of this great actor better than by quoting some portions of his farewell address, which he delivered at the " Wells" on that memorable night of November 6th, 1862, after eighteen years of heroic effort to make the Shakespearian drama known and appreciated with its centre of illustration in such a neighbourhood as Islington. The address will explain the great suceess of his efforts. He said :—

" Most of you doubtless are aware that formerly by virtue of their patents, Drury Lane, Covent Garden, and the Haymarket were the only Theatres allowed to act Shakespeare, and the high-class Drama usually termed legitimate. The restrictions preventing other Theatres from doing so were removed, and after some consideration, myself and Mrs. Warner issued an address to the public."

.   .   .   .   .

" In a short time Mrs. Warner withdrew and I was left alone in the Management. I at once determined to make it the object of my life and the end of the management to represent the whole of Shakespeare's plays. I have succeeded in placing upon the stage thirty-four of them, and they have been acted between three and four thousand nights."

.   .   .   .   .   .

" The production of thirty-four plays of Shakespeare, some of which have been considered unactable, is a feat, I believe, never before attempted by any manager, at least in modern times. It has been to me a labour of love—an object of pride, rather than a source of profit, for when I tell you that the single play of " Pericles " cost in its pro duction £1,000 and the expense lavished upon the others being very great, you will easily perceive how impossible it was in such a Th eatre as this that my labour should be rewarded by large pecuniary profit."

.   .   .   .   .   .

" Before I conclude allow me to observe how much I have been gratified in having been the means of bringing to this house, a large body of young men—men, most of whom have received their first theatrical impressions in witnessing the plays of Shakespeare. The amusements of the people are a most important item in the composition of our Social System. Dramatic representations have, and, I believe, in some form or other always will stand in the fore-most rank of those amusements ; and it is surely better that the young, who are so easily and strongly impressed by them, should receive those impressions from the plays of Shakepeare, rather than from sen sational dramas or translations from the French of question-able morality. And now having long endeavoured to deserve your respect, I feel that I leave you accompanied by good wishes, to some future sc ene of action, and respectfully bid you—Farewell."

CHAPTER IV.

CHARLES ALEXANDER CALVERT.

IT is difficult, when writing of the life and work of
Charles Calvert, who was a dear and delightful
friend, to keep within moderate bounds of praise and
appreciation.   Such friendships, as existed between us,
are precious, and build up memories which are pleasant
and enduring as long as life lasts.

In my allusions to the great work of Calvert,
which has left its mark in the historic annals of the
Victorian stage, I will faithfully record its result and
effect on the art of the theatre in the latter half of the
last century, and on that of the present time.

My recollections of Charles Calvert date back from
the year 1861, when, amidst the interest attending the
volunteer movement, it was decided by the architects
and civil engineers of Manchester to establish a corps
as part and parcel of the regiments of the town and
district.   An amateur performance was arranged,
(towards raising the funds) of " As You Like It," and
"High Life Below Stairs."   This took place at the

Theatre Royal under Calvert's supervision, and friend-ships arose between architects, artists and engineers, and with the genial manager of the Theatre Royal, which only ended with life itself.

It was, however, in 1864, with the opening of the new Prince's Theatre in Oxford Street, that the serious and enthusiastic work of Calvert's life commenced. It is a curious thing that the City of Manchester, the leading town of the provinces, should have become the centre of all that was noble and beautiful in the exposition of Shakespearean drama after the metropolitan efforts of Charles Kean and Samuel Phelps had ceased. It must not be assumed that Shakespeare was dead to the metropolis; but the continuance of the grand exposition of his work was carried on in a provincial city in a superior manner, with increased knowledge, and unlimited finance; the cope-stone of effort was placed upon the beautiful edifice raised by the metro-politan managers, to whose work I have already alluded.

There are persons living who remember that eventful evening of October 15th, 1864, when the new Prince's Theatre opened with his first revival of "The Tempest." I venture to think that that event was of vital importance in the history of our local and national stage. That night inaugurated a policy from which, in spite of adverse criticism and prophecy of financial disaster, Manager Calvert never swerved or departed in the slightest degree. "The Tempest" was produced with beautiful scenery, good acting, good music (will the episode of dear Julia St. George singing "Where the Bee Sucks," time after time, ever be forgotten by those who were present?) in fact, everything was as good as money and brains could produce. It would require whole volumes to give anything like a complete history of the work which illustrated Calvert's policy of Shakespearean production. I will therefore rest content with allusions to the main features of that work; and to its influence on the world of art and culture.

It may be well to enumerate the "Revivals" in order of time. I have just said the theatre was opened with the "Tempest" in 1864. This was followed, in 1865, by "Much Ado about Nothing;" "A Midsummer Night's Dream" was produced in the same year, "Anthony and Cleopatra" in 1866, "Winter's Tale" in 1869, "Richard III." in 1870, "Timon of Athens" in 1871, "Merchant of Venice" also in 1871, "Henry V." in 1872, "Twelfth Night" in 1873, and "Henry IV." (Second Part) in 1874. "Henry VIII." was Calvert's last Shakespearean revival at the Theatre Royal, after he had severed his connection with the Prince's Theatre.

As I have said, the opening of the new Prince's Theatre, in Manchester, in 1864, was of vital importance in the history, not only of the local, but of the national stage. A number of cultured gentlemen and capitalists induced Charles Calvert to leave the management of the Theatre Royal, throw in his lot with the new venture, and to take the reins of management.

This opportunity was embraced by Mr. Calvert without hesitation, for he saw a prospect of gratifying an ambition always in his mind, namely, to produce the works of Shakespeare, and the modern high-class drama, in a scholarly and worthy manner.

This combination of brains and capital resulted in the brightest epoch in the history of the provincial stage, and was regarded by the artistic and literary world as a monumental effort to maintain the dignity, the beauty, and the grandeur of the greatest dramatic works, to uphold the honourable position of the theatre, and to elevate the general tone of the stage.

The *raison d'être* of the Prince's Theatre venture was well expressed in the opening address, written by my friend, H. M. Acton, and spoken by Mr. Calvert, a portion of which may be appropriately quoted :—

> On our side, too, perhaps some ancient claims
> May pass as warrant for our present aims?
> If so, believe no purpose, light or vain,
> Rears to the Drama this its last-built fane.
> Here we aspire, you aiding us, to lend
> The Art we live for to its worthiest end ;
> To bid the grand old masters of our craft
> Speak as though still they lived ; abroad to waft
> The words of wisdom, charity, and wit,
> Which Shakespeare, Sheridan, and Goldsmith writ ;
> Nor yet neglect whate'er the modern age
> And living talent yield to grace the stage.
> So may we hope the generous mind to reach
> With sweetened lore, and, pleasing, still to teach ;
> Alike at Virtue's and the Muses' call
> To bid the alternate passions rise and fall ;—

The mirth that asks from modesty no blush ;
Tears that from Nature's kindliest fountains gush ;
And deeper grave those lessons on the mind,
Which, while they charm, instruct and warn mankind.
A great ambition ! but if you assist,
Hard though our toil, its aim will not be miss'd ;
And, think ! if, haply, in some future year,
Children of yours seek chastened pleasure here,
How just the pride, if honour then be due,
To feel no trifling share belongs to you !
Yours, generous patrons ! were the eyes to mark
When from the shore first crept our modest bark ;
You saw its form, and deemed its promise good ;
You helped its trembling passage to the flood,
And sped it bounding, in a worthy cause,
Before the favouring gale of your applause !

To write the history of the Manchester Prince's
Theatre under the Calvert régime would involve a task
far exceeding the limits of this work; therefore I
must rest content with an abbreviated history, with
especial reference to that portion of it with which I
was more intimately associated. It must be admitted
by everyone acquainted with the history of the modern
English stage, that the work done by Calvert in the
Provinces was valued and respected by the artistic
and cultured patrons of the Drama throughout the
country; and during a period of ten years the little
Prince's Theatre was the home of legitimate art, and
the abiding place of the Shakespearean drama.
It is true that Charles Kean and Samuel Phelps
were the pioneers in the great work of Shakespearian
production; but the developments made under the

Calvert "Revivals" in Manchester, and since carried beyond the most sanguine expectations by the late great actor-manager, Sir Henry Irving, have caused the earlier efforts to fade almost away into the historic past; and there are only a few old playgoers who remember them, and from whom any detailed account can be obtained.

At the outset of his work, Calvert adopted the dictum of the late Cardinal Wiseman: that Shakespeare wrote *to be acted*, and *not to be read*.

From that memorable night of October 15th, 1864, when the Prince's Theatre doors opened with "The Tempest," revived on Calvert's principles, to the date of the last "revival" of "Henry IV." (second part) in 1874, playgoers had the satisfaction and enjoyment of a brilliant epoch in the history of the stage—an epoch which brought *prestige* and profit to those who had had the courage to expend time and money on what was predicted would be a disastrous undertaking. The true keynote was struck on the opening night: I venture to think that that event was of vital importance in the history of the Manchester stage. As I have already said, I cannot attempt anything like a complete history of the work which illustrated Calvert's policy of Shakespearean production. I will therefore rest content with a few allusions to the main features of that work, and to its influence on the world of art and culture.

In the production of "The Tempest" Calvert had to deal with what was purely artistic both in scenery

and costume. After the first fine effect of the ship-
wreck, the landscape artist was supreme, and revelled
in the depiction of the poetic landscape of "The Enchanted Island." The imagination of the poet was
reflected in the exquisite and masterly work of Grieve
and Holding. In addition to scenic effort, was the
beautiful music by Purcell, Dr. Arne, and Arthur
Sullivan, which filled the Isle with sweet sound. The
acting of the whole piece was excellent, and when
William Beverley's beautiful act drop descended, the
audience felt they had entered on a new lease of
artistic theatrical life, and gave expression to the fact
in rounds of applause.

The two following productions of "Much Ado
About Nothing" and "A Midsummer Night's Dream"
were conducted on similar lines with equal success;
but in the third revival, "Antony and Cleopatra" was
opened up a fresh source of interest and investigation.
It was essential that the poetry of the work should be
enshrined in the architecture of its historic period, and
that the living representations of the poet's fancy
should be clothed according to the time of the reign
of the great Egyptian Queen, and of the people of
whom the great Roman was the representative. In
"Antony and Cleopatra" everything was achieved by
a lavish expenditure of art, knowledge, and money. It
was a wonderful production with its quaint old-world
architecture, its revels under the shades of Philæ, its
Augustan grandeur, and its Egyptian mysticism.
Tom Taylor, whose opinion on matters connected

with the art of the stage I always valued, wrote his opinion of the work in a letter to the "Manchester Guardian," in which he said:

"As a dramatic writer, practically conversant for more than a quarter of a century with the stage, stage production, and stage management, and as one who in the course of the last thirty years, has followed with interest the revivals of Shakespeare's plays by Macready at Covent Garden, and Drury Lane, and by Charles Kean at the Princess's, I hope I may venture, without impertinence, to express under my own name, the surprise and gratification with which I last week saw Mr. Calvert's revival of "Antony and Cleopatra" at the Prince's Theatre. I but record my unexaggerated conviction when I say, that in judgment, liberality, and good taste,—apart from the signal merit of the performance of the principal parts— this revival appeared to me quite deserving to rank with the best of those of Macready and Charles Kean.

"Feeling grateful to Mr. Calvert for the pleasure he has given me, I feel it a reflected credit for Manchester, that it should be made the scene of such a theatrical venture. As one whose theatrical fortunes are most intimately bound up with London theatres, and London managements, I can only wish that we had in the Metropolis more of the spirit which, judging by this revival, does not despair of recognition and reward in this great seat of manufacturing industry."

Helen Faucit (Lady Martin) wrote: "I may sincerely

say that, neither at home or abroad, have I seen a play put upon the stage more satisfactorily in all its details of scenery, grouping, and costume."

These expressions of opinion determined Calvert to continue the line of action he adopted when the Prince's Theatre opened its doors. He foresaw the attainment of a *prestige* for theatrical enterprise, of which he was the "head and front"—a *prestige* which, I venture to say, has never been attained by any provincial theatre of our time. In the early years of the theatre it was worked under the auspices of a limited company, and the Directors stood loyally by the Manager in the line of policy he had adopted. Calvert called to his aid such artists and scholars as Grieve, Telbin, Alma Tadema, R.A., J. D. Watson, Rawdon Brown, and Arthur Sullivan. The musical director was the late Alfred Cellier, genius and delightful gentleman, whose memory we dearly treasure.

The production of the " Merchant of Venice " illustrated Calvert's enthusiasm, and the confidence that was placed in the policy he was pursuing. He was sent to Venice—where he gathered a mass of material and local colouring, purchased and brought home a gondola (afterwards transferred to the waters of the Thames),—and everything that trouble, research, and money could do was done in honour of this immortal play. It was in this revival that Calvert realised one of those artistic master-strokes which took the art-world by storm, so to speak, and cast a halo of poetry over the piece which still lives sweetly in the memory.

Portia's last speech begins—" It is almost morning,"
and on these few words Calvert built up a result that
was fascinating in its beauty. At the end of the
speech the pages went round and quietly extinguished
the lights ; the guests dispersed to the sounds of song
and music ; the scene became gradually empty, dark,
and silent ; and the curtain slowly fell. This was a
bold stroke of stage art, but it was exquisite in its
quiet beauty. The audience dispersed with a con-
sciousness that their hearts had been gladdened and
drawn very closely towards the genius of the immortal
dramatist. The power and beauty of the work were
made apparent, and a feeling of thankfulness was
expressed in the applause which burst forth for the
manager who was doing so much in honour of the
great master.

As time went on, the policy pursued by Calvert
became so popular, that the little Prince's Theatre
was found inadequate to accommodate the increasing
audiences. It was accordingly determined by the
Directorate that the house should be enlarged. I
was called in to devise a scheme by which the house
should be stretched to its utmost capacity ; thus commenced my professional association with the architecture of the theatre. The alterations were very
extensive, and somewhat difficult of attainment. I
was instructed to provide an additional circle without
raising the roof, and to construct a new proscenium.
I was allowed *carte-blanche* in the decoration ; but the
scheme was to be in accordance with the Shake-

spearean idea of the management. I accordingly induced H. Stacy Marks, R.A., to paint a proscenium
frieze, the subject being Shakespeare enthroned
between Tragedy and Comedy, and attended on
either side by representative figures from the principal
plays. This picture is one of the finest decorative
paintings of our times, and retains its beauty and
freshness to the present day. The box fronts were
adorned by medallion portraits of the principal tragic
characters, with incidents from the plays, all painted
by William Phillips. Colour was freely introduced
to balance these decorative pictures; and what was
admitted to be the prettiest theatre in the country
was opened on the 6th of August, 1869, with a
production of "Much Ado about Nothing."

When Calvert entered on his first revival of one of
Shakespeare's works founded on mediæval English
history, a new line of investigation was opened, and
classicism surrendered to mediævalism. In "Richard
III.," "Henry IV.," and "Henry V.," a phase of
scenery, costume, and armour, was placed upon the
stage in a manner and completeness never before
achieved.

Calvert's greatest, and I think his favourite, work
was "Henry V.," produced in 1872. In this revival
he reached the zenith of his managerial efforts. In
recording Calvert's work, I may remark that he not
only desired to please the eye and delight the ear, but
he strove to make his revivals educational; consequently he found in "Henry V." an opportunity of

illustrating the life and manners of mediæval England, and the "pomp and circumstance" of mediæval warfare. In short, that period of English history was displayed on the stage immediately before the advent of the Renaissance under the Tudors. It was the epoch of plate armour, flowing robes, picturesque architecture, and of that pictorial splendour which could appropriately be cast around Shakespeare's favourite hero.

I had the good fortune to be intimately associated with my friend in this celebrated revival. When this work was in contemplation, I happened to be resident at Marple Hall, in Cheshire, formerly the home of Bradshaw, the regicide, and it was in this house, surrounded by armour, tapestry, old pictures, and quaint furniture, that I planned out and designed the architectural scenes; and it was here also that I conceived the idea of realising the correct blazon of the arms and banners, as they were actually used on the heroic field of Agincourt. Calvert would spend hours with me in the gloomy old mansion, and would pace about its rooms and corridors in delightful restlessness and excitement, as I described and explained my portion of the work. Calvert seemed as though he could not rest content until he saw the idea in some tangible shape, either on paper or in modelled form. On my return to Manchester, I commenced the practical working out of the duties I had undertaken.

It is difficult to convey a true idea of the amount of trouble, research, and anxiety involved by this revival of " Henry V. ' A faithful historical picture of the period of the early part of the 15th century had to be realised. The architecture and the scenery had to be as nearly as possible reproductions of the streets of London, the seaport of Southampton, the walled town of Harfleur, the battle-field of Agincourt, the Palaces of Westminster and Rouen, and the Cathedral of Troyes. The costumes were made from a series of beautiful drawings by that master of pictorial habiliments, the late J. D. Watson. Watson's enthusiasm knew no bounds : he not only made his careful drawings from best authorities, but he would actually cut out the patterns to ensure correctness and exactitude ; and personally superintended the work of the costumier. The most difficult scene to represent was "The Entry into London," described by "Chorus." In this case it was necessary to follow the accounts of the old chroniclers of the period ; not only had the architecture of old London to be reproduced, but the decorations and incidents which constituted " The Pageant." Metrical histories, Harleian MSS., and all the available sources of information had to be consulted before the scene model could be made. Many practical difficulties had to be overcome ; the "wings" and "flats" were of such a height and size that they had to be hinged in several flaps for convenience of movement, and for transmission to other countries. When that great scene was set up and lighted, everybody felt satisfied and repaid for the trouble and expense it had involved. The scene settled on, the entry and incidents of the pageant had to be realised.

The patrons of the theatre have no idea of the difficulty a manager experiences in drilling a crowd of "supers." The "super" is an individual, as a rule, without intellectuality; in fact, if he had any, he would not be a super. It was only by incessant drilling that the crowd of soldiers and the mass of London citizens could be got to do the right thing at the right moment. There is an amusing story told which illustrates the quality of the "super" mind. When "Faust" was being prepared by Sir Henry Irving at the Lyceum, the idea of the "Brocken" scene had to be carried into practical effect; after some trouble the leading idea of the scene was firmly planted in the brain of the "super master." He then proceeded to drill his men in squads, and worked hard till the rehearsal of the complete scene. After weeks of labour, what was the result? The witches rushed on exactly in the style of frolicsome pantomimic demons. The super master was simply horrified; he shouted at the top of his voice, "No! No!! No!!! No!!!! not so 'appy, not so 'appy, go back—you're not on 'ampstead 'eath, you're in 'ell!"

The entry into London in "Henry V." contained between two and three hundred persons; but on the first night they were perfect, and all went "merry as a marriage bell." There are old playgoers who still have pleasant memories of this great scene. To me it was the realisation of an ideal: it represented all that art and stagecraft could do to illustrate a great historical poem. Those who saw the scene will not have forgotten the crowd of citizens, artizans, youths, maidens and nobles of the land who filled the streets and temporary balconies hung with tapestries, and who with eager expectation awaited the arrival of the young King-hero at the entrance to London Bridge. One remembers the distant hum of voices, and how the volume of sound swelled as the little army approached on its march from Blackheath ; how the sound burst into a mighty shout as the hero of Agincourt rode through the triumphal archway, the "Deo gratius Anglia redde pro victoria" and other hymns of praise filled the air, showers of gold dust fell from the turrets, red roses of Lancaster covered the rude pavements, the bells clashed out, and a great thanksgiving went up to heaven for the preservation of the gallant King and his little army of heroes. The curtain descended on a perfect picture of mediæval England. If any doubts existed as to the proper method of producing the plays of Shakespeare, this revival of " Henry V." removed them, and settled the question beyond argument.

I have said that Charles Calvert's revivals were educational in their scope as well as dramatic. In " Henry V." I made an effort to display the heraldry of the time ; and the banners, shields, and other devices actually used at Agincourt were, after much labour and research, faithfully reproduced. In the process of investigation, certain points in English heraldry, about which doubts had existed, were set at rest and settled, and for the first time the Agincourt roll-of-arms was blazoned. It cannot be doubted that this production of "Henry V." in Manchester was an event of importance in stage history. The annals of the stage will record the production of this piece in America, under Calvert's personal supervision, at Booth's Theatre, New York, on Feb. 8th, 1875, and the immense success it achieved. The *Boston Herald* wrote: "More than 100,000 persons have already visited Booth's Theatre to enjoy the magnificent revival of "Henry V.," and there is thus far no perceptible diminution in the size of the audience."

If I were writing a life of Charles Calvert (which I am not), I could insert letters of the greatest interest which I received from him during his visit to America, wherein the difficulties he experienced on producing the piece are detailed. It is a matter of history in stage annals how George Rignold carried the production through the States and into Australia, and that immense sums of money were taken by its exhibition, till it finally disappeared from the stage, with my old scenery worn out, and the proudly-waving banners of Agincourt tattered and torn till their devices were beyond recognition.

I may here appropriately insert some extracts from Calvert's farewell address, delivered on the last night of "Henry V." He said:—

This night is the end of a memorable event, and in reviewing the results of this our latest effort, I see three special reasons for mutual exultation—the success in every sense of the production, the enlarging taste for the works of the greatest dramatist that ever lived, and the indisputable fact that the ignorant prejudice against the theatre as an institution is declining, I feel assured that these three truths are as gratifying to you as they are to me, and although at this moment it is your good pleasure to direct your approval towards your humble servant, still the chief merit rests with you ; for had you not supported and encouraged us we should have reaped nothing but the consolation that we had suffered in a good cause. But this night marks the accomplishment of one of the greatest Shakesperian triumphs that has ever been known in the history of Art. A greater amount of money has been paid to obtain admission to the performance of " Henry V.," and a greater display of enthusiasm has been shown regarding the play than can be recorded in our previous annals. I ask you who, by your oft-repeated visits to these representations, have testified that to Shakespeare at the Prince's Theatre you owe many and many an evening of keen enjoyment, to bear your testimony to the certain truth, that that inspired man has not written in vain ; nor should the stage of our country, that he so graced by his genius, be denounced as a vain thing.

.   .   .   .   .   .

I appreciate very highly the honour you do me this night. My crown of "borrowed majesty" I now give up. My court is dismissed ; my soldiers disbanded and their bows unstrung ; and all our glories fade from your view ; but I hope not from your memories. The laurels you bestow on me by your applause, and by your hearty and enthusiastic patronage during the seventy-four representations of the play, you will, I am sure, allow me to share with my brothers and sisters in art, and to whom I am indebted for a zealous and hearty co-operation, and who are now assembled in some numbers behind this curtain, and anxious with me to bow their acknowledgments of the honours you this night confer.

Amid the applause which greeted this address the curtain rose, discovering the whole company, who

siezed the opportunity of testifying their appreciation
of their manager by a hearty round of cheering.
Thus "Henry V." and all his mimic surrounding
passed away into history of the Manchester theatrical
enterprise.

I have said that it is not part of my scheme to
write a life of Charles Calvert. I cannot, however,
dismiss the portion of my life story with which he was
associated, without some allusion to his managerial
work outside its Shakespearean phase. The popu-
larity of the Prince's Theatre was so great that it was
a matter of ease to command the best talent in the
profession, and to secure the best theatrical attractions.
To enumerate all the successful engagements made
by Calvert would occupy more space than I can spare,
but the most successful, both financially and artistically,
were those made with Jefferson, Emmett, Nielson,
Toole, and Phelps.

Calvert's mind was cast in a mystical and physico-
logical mould : this mental condition was fostered and
cultivated by his study and contemplation of the
writings of Swedenborg ; it will not, therefore, be a
matter of surprise that the dramatic work of Lord
Byron had a strange fascination for him. He produced " The Two Foscari," a gruesome play never
before given on the stage ; and he took a strange
delight in presenting the weird play of " Manfred" to
his Manchester patrons. Both these, although beautifully given, were not popular ; but he was destined to
achieve a success with " Sardanapalus," which was

first produced at the Alexandra Theatre, Liverpool,
after his association with the Prince's Theatre had
ceased. Louisa Moore was the Myrrha, and the late
Frederick Clay wrote some original music, barbaric in
character, and conducted the orchestra on the first
performance of the piece. I shall never forget that
first night; the burning of the palace was so realistic
that the audience took alarm, and had to be quieted by
an explanation from the stage.

"After the adieu to Assyria, Sardanapalus mounts
the pile, and stands by the throne"; this is the stage
direction in Calvert's acting edition of the play. The
last words are spoken by Myrrha. "'Tis fired! I
come!" Then the final stage direction runs thus :—

"As Myrrha springs up the pile to join the king,
the flames suddenly break forth, surround and seem
to devour them, the whole mass becomes a huge
conflagration ; great volumes of smoke roll across the
stage ; the columns are heard to fall and crumble ; the
pyre sinks ; the roof falls ; the walls of the palace give
way, disclosing the distance ; and after a time, the
clouds of smoke clearing off, the palace is seen a heap
of ruins." As the proof-sheets of the play came to
hand, Calvert would insist on my reading them to
him; I caught his enthusiasm, and readily entered
into all his proposals for the mounting of the play.
When, however, the final catastrophe was reached, I
recoiled at his realistic propositions. His reply was,
"Don't be alarmed, my boy! the play is a poem over
the heads of the people, but the 'conflagration' will

make it a *financial* success." Such was the fact;
"Sardanapalus" went through the country, and reaped
a golden harvest.

A trait in Calvert's character strongly developed
was a love of his fellow-man. A tale of trouble or
suffering affected him deeply. In 1871, after that
dreadful Franco-German war, subscriptions were got
up in the country to alleviate the sufferings of its
victims. Calvert conceived the idea of a series of
Stage Tableaux or living pictures, which should
illustrate the horrors of war, the sufferings entailed,
and the blessings of peace. The first exhibition of
these pictures took place at the Prince's Theatre, on
February 6th, 1871. Here is the Programme :—

1st TABLEAU : "Summoned to the War."
2nd   „   "Another Sortie."
3rd   ..   "The Prayer in the Church."
4th   „   "War." ⎫
5th   „   "Peace." ⎬ After *Landseer.*
6th   „   "An Allegorical Tableau," in
which Mr. CHARLES CALVERT will appear as
"PEACE," and deliver an Ode.
FINAL TABLEAU :
"THE DOVE AND THE OLIVE BRANCH."

The success of this event was extraordinary ; a
morning performance of the Tableaux had to be given,
and, after paying all costs connected therewith, there
was at the disposal of the " War Victims' Fund " a
sum of over £300.*

* I allude to this Stage Tableaux Entertainment because it was beautiful
and artistic, and formed another illustration of the high art of the stage in
the Victorian Era.

In 1875 Calvert left the scene of his managerial triumphs in Manchester and produced "Sardanapalus," as I have said, in Liverpool. In 1877 he revived " Henry VIII." in grand style at the Theatre Royal, Manchester. This was the last of his great Shakespearean Revivals, and in which he sustained the part of Wolsey with marked success.

Calvert was never a strong man physically, and those who knew him well often saw indications of failing health. He carried " Henry V." to Birmingham, and it was in that city that the first serious break-down occurred, in 1873. On the first night it was evident he was suffering from severe indisposition, and, on uttering the line, " Oh ! God of Battles, steel my soldiers' hearts," he suddenly stopped, swooned, and was carried from the stage in what appeared a dying condition. The curtain fell on one of the most painful scenes ever witnessed in a theatre. The run of the piece continued, with Mr. Reginald Moore as the King. Calvert slowly recovered, but the rest of his career was characterised by broken and uncertain health.

The last years of Charles Calvert's life form a melancholy record. I was the last of the old circle to see him at Fulham, where he was under careful medical treatment ; but he died in a few days after my visit, on the 12th June, 1879, at the age of 51.

The late Mrs. Alexander Ireland (author of the " Life of Jane Welsh Carlyle "), in her " Lives of Manchester Men and Women," has written of Calvert:

"Charles Calvert was a man we could ill spare, and those who can look back and remember what the 'Prince's Theatre was in his days will acknowledge that we lost in him a stage manager unrivalled for resource, organisation, and the weightier qualities of scholarly research and historical accuracy. Add to these an inborn artistic gift, a fine cultivated mind, and deep powers of spiritual conception, and you will have some idea of what he was "!

Charles Calvert was laid to rest in the Brooklands Cemetery on the 18th of June. The long cortège came from the station, paused before the Theatre Royal, and the hearse drew up for a few moments opposite the facade of the Prince's Theatre. I shall never forget that dense crowd, that sea of human faces, standing silent and grave. The tears welled into the eyes at such a tribute to the man, and the art he had taught those masses of Lancashire people to love and honour. A London paper described the scene in these words : " Between Manchester and the Brooklands Cemetery, where lie the mortal remains of Charles Alexander Calvert, no fewer than 50,000 people had assembled to pay their friend and teacher the last tribute of respect in their power to offer. It is in this peaceful spot that he rests, after a long and honourable life, the effects of which happily yet remain, and may be distinctly traced in many of the theatres to which he had at different times devoted his attention."

The funeral oration at the grave side was an impromptu effort, and so admirable that it is inserted

here as an honourable tribute to the memory of
Charles Alexander Calvert, and a recognition of his
grand efforts to elevate and to honour the art of the
Victorian Stage :

The frame which is now consigned to its grave must have been
much beloved in its frequent appearances before men and women to
have commanded this mighty audience this afternoon to tender the
last tribute of affection and regard. It is very true, if I am not
impertinent in saying so, that we come to bury Calvert, not to praise
him. He must have had a large hold upon the hearts and affections
of men and women, not only here, but very likely throughout the
length and breadth of the British Empire, too. That he was much
beloved and much honoured, surely this audience before me attests
and witnesses. It is often supposed that there is a sharp line of
demarcation between the profession of the minister and the Christian
profession of that of the great actor. I don't know why it should be
thought so exactly, for it seems to me that whoever he may be who
impersonates noble emotions and lofty conceptions—whoever he may
be who imparts innocent and cheerful mirth, must be regarded as a
great public benefactor ; and in the memory of this, we may say that
a great public benefactor has gone, and gone unexpectedly, from our
midst. All genius is from God. The power to interpret great ideas,
the power to impersonate noble emotions, no less than the power
which expresses them, we are to conceive is derived from God, who
is the giver of every great and good gift. We cannot but know that
he whom we are interring to-day has really stirred and aroused noble
feelings and impressions to the hearts and minds of men. I have had
conveyed to my mind also the knowledge while I have been coming
here that he was not less a man of religious convictions and religious
impressions, although perhaps, not finding their solution in some of
those which are regarded as the ordinary and popular forms of such
ideas. However that may be, the mighty impersonater of death
is dead. The mighty and masterly tragedian has yielded to that
tragedy to which at last we shall all have to yield, the great tragedy

which closes life—death ! Through a painful illness, through a complication of painful diseases such as have been described to me, he has found that the best physician is death—death from which we shrink back and shudder all our lives, but which that great spirit whose words he was so fond of interpreting and quoting has told us is

"As a lover's pinch,
Which hurts, and is desir'd."

Well, now then we leave him here in the midst of this presence of duty, beneath that blue sky, in the midst of the glories and pomp of these trees, with their green and gold, and in the beauty of this sunshine ; but we do not leave him altogether in the grasp of Nature. We do not leave him there at all. Whatever lived of Calvert, lives. It is not possible that the spirit which can stir noble sentiments or express noble thoughts can pass away as something which resolves itself into dust, but as no more. The immortal spirit lives, and I shall believe that through the faith which we have in Jesus Christ our Lord, who says, "Come unto me all ye who labour and are heavy laden, and I will give you rest ;" who tells us, or of whom we are told, that it was His province to bring life and immortality to light through His gospel. With these pleasant hopes, with these bright and cheerful sentiments, we now consign to the grave this beloved brother and dear neighbour and townsman of yours, whose last wish was that he should repose in this beautiful cemetery. We leave him here in the full and assured hope that, as he lives among the spirits yonder in the light and love of the world to come, those who long to meet him again shall meet him on the morrow.

On the Brooklands gravestone I had the words cut—

"After life's fitful fever he sleeps well."

With Calvert's death was closed one of the most delightful artistic experiences of my lifetime.

My professional association with the Manchester

Prince's Theatre for many years brought me into pleasant contact with the men and women who stood loyally by the side of their manager, and who assisted his work by their intelligent and artistic impersonation of the many parts comprised in the stage productions. It would occupy too much space were I to even attempt allusions to all the actors and actresses who worked with Charles Calvert; but their names and parts will be found in the Appendix to this work.

I must, however, make allusion to those who played important parts in the *modus operandi* of producing the Shakespearean and high class drama. First and foremost I must allude to Mrs. Calvert. It is a curious fact that the managers who added lustre to the art work of the Victorian Stage were materially assisted and encouraged by their wives; and Charles Calvert was blessed by a helpmate who added grace and dignity to the impersonation of the principal female parts in the revivals of the Shakespearean drama. Mrs. Calvert, standing in robes of white and laurel, wreathed as Chorus in " Henry V." is a picture that will, along with her fine delivery of the beautiful lines of the great master, ever constitute a delightful memory. Although it is beyond the scope of this work to deal with the stage art of the Edwardian Era I cannot resist offering my tribute of praise and thanks to the highly gifted woman who is giving fresh life to the matronly women in the revivals of our old comedies, and who invigorates the modern comedy work of our time with point, power, and originality of

treatment. Mrs. Charles Calvert is the interesting
and historic link between the great period of the art of
the Victorian stage, and the best stage art of the
present time. I am not mistaken when I say that
what is called the " new school " of histrionic art owes
much to the talented lady who thoroughly understood
the art and *raison d'être* of the best stage work of the
Victorian Theatre.

In Calvert's work scenic and musical illustration
played important parts in stage production in association with costume, armour, heraldry, and stage
management. Men of high distinction were consulted,
and their advice was followed both in classic and
mediæval display. Calvert, like Charles Kean, adopted
the plan of publishing the acting version of each of his
revivals, quoting his authorities in prefatory remarks,
and not on fly-leaves attached to the play-bills. These
are interesting to the student of archæology and will
always remain interesting for future reference.

In addition to the artists of high repute before
mentioned, the names of two musicians must be
recorded on the historic scroll of the art of the
Victorian Stage. Alfred Cellier and Sir Arthur
Sullivan contributed largely to the completeness of
Charles Calvert's great revivals at the theatres in
Manchester. Cellier had the good fortune to find in
Calvert a manager who could recognize good art in
any form, and, consequently, the future author of
" Dorothy " found an appropriate medium of expres-
sion for his " Sultan of Mocha," " Tower of London,"

"Nell Gwynne," and "Belladonna." It was a brilliant period for music as long as Alfred Cellier remained conductor of the orchestra for Charles Calvert; personally he was loved by all with whom he came in contact, either in business or in society, and his memory is dearly cherished by those who survive him. Sir Arthur Sullivan did much original incidental work for the Calvert revivals; Calvert's revival of " Henry VIII." at the Manchester Theatre Royal was remarkable for the Sullivan music, which enhanced the scenic charm of such episodes as the sail down the river to the christening of the infant princess. Sullivan enjoyed being associated with Calvert in his artistic and scholarly efforts to raise the tone and quality of the art of the stage. With Sullivan's death, the world of art lost a genius, and the Victorian Stage a devotee, unique in its annals.

In order to show the high appreciation of Calvert's work for the stage, I cannot do better than include a record of the Memorial Performances held in the year of his death in October, 1879. I confess that when the matter came to be discussed and arranged, I was not only surprised, but delighted at the eager desire of men, renowned in art and literature, to help in a testimonial founded on amateur effort.

As one of the executors of the late Mr. Calvert, I deemed it desirable that the public should have some opportunity of showing respect for his memory, and at the same time, of making some substantial addition to the funds at the disposal of the trustees for the benefit of his bereaved family. With this object in view I determined to consult the late Mr. Tom Taylor, the well-known dramatic author and at that period the editor of *Punch*. Mr. Taylor's acquaintance I made in 1873, when he came to Manchester to try his experiment of mounting " Hamlet " after the fashion in which it was played in Shakespeare's time. He invited me to meet the late Steele Mackye, to talk over the idea, and the piece was produced in Manchester, with Mackye as the Prince of Denmark. Mr. Taylor also consented to preside at the banquet given to Mr. Calvert, prior to his departure for America to produce " Henry V." His speech was an eloquent tribute to the cultured and artistic manager, and the affair passed off with considerable enthusiasm. I felt that if Mr. Taylor would enter into the project, success was certain. And so it was. We hit upon the idea of performing a Shakespearean Comedy, the cast of which should be composed of those literary men, musicians, and artists who had been associated in any way with Calvert's great work at the Prince's Theatre, Manchester.

The project was discussed in London, and at Tom Taylor's delightful home at " Lavender Sweep." I returned to Manchester, and organised a committee, which was important and representative in character, including 125 names of local men of note, and the names of Metropolitan managers and leading actors, authors and dramatists.

The forming of this great committee was a matter

of ease—everybody was anxious to be associated with the event; but the getting up of the performance was quite a different matter. It was an experience that a man would not care to have twice in a lifetime. In the matter of the committee, everybody was content to appear in alphabetical order; but in the matter of the performance, everybody seemed to want to play the best parts, and everybody wanted to be stage manager. There were two Rosalinds in the field, and two versions of the play, and the prompter stood a chance of becoming a hopeless lunatic before those two memorable nights were ended.

Although the raison d'être of those memorable performances to many of us was sad, the humours and adventures were curious, of which I have written fully in my "Book of Experiences."

As I am introducing into this work a notice of the "Calvert Memorial Performances," I will confine my remarks to such points as will illustrate the extra-ordinary influence gained by Calvert through his work on the artistic and cultured minds of the country.

It was soon decided that the only Shakespearean Comedy that amateurs could approach was "As You Like It," and I was made responsible for the produc-tion and cast of the piece. As I write, I am saddened as I note how many of those clever men, and dear friends, have "gone to that bourn from whence no traveller returns"; I trust my record will wound nobody living, and I shall certainly "set down naught in malice," although I may not extenuate some of the amateur faults of the dead.

Shall I ever forget the worry and anxiety of the three months occupied in organising these memorial performances?—I think not; as I write, I seem to live the anxious time over again; and the wonder is how it was got through, and with such a successful result. Mr. Tom Taylor was a tower of strength to me, and my good friend, the late Hon. Lewis Wingfield, novelist, playwright, and critic, stood manfully by our side through all the trials, difficulties, and disappointments which beset us.

At the outset two "tyrannic thoughts" took possession of my mind. One was, that if we could enlist the help of the *Punch* staff we should be certain of success; and and other was that if Lady Martin (Helen Faucit) could be induced to come from her retirement and play Rosalind, success would be doubly sure, and the event would become historic in the annals of the stage. The latter idea was realised; the former partially.

A circular including the cast of distinguished names for parts in "As You Like It" was issued; as may be imagined, this caused quite a sensation. Applications for tickets poured in from London, and other parts of the country, and so hopeless appeared the task of allotting places that the Committee determined to open the box office on a certain day for places to be secured in the ordinary way.

Great interest was attached to the event, which

was rendered memorable in stage annals by the fact of
Helen Faucit (Lady Martin) coming from her retirement to play her favourite heroine, Rosalind, to show
her high respect for the memory of the man who had
done so much for the artistic production of the
Shaksperean drama. I remember the excitement in
the city reached almost fever heat when the announce-
ment was made that she would play. I should imagine
that the rush for seats at the Theatre Royal was
unprecedented in its history.

The rehearsals dwell in my memory as curious
experiences. In this crowd of distinguished men
there seemed two elements of trouble and disaster.
Herman Merivale and Tom Taylor, being used to the
stage and its conventionalities through the production
of their own dramas, assumed a right to "boss" the
"show," to which the professional ladies objected.
Then, again, some of those amateurs were absolutely
ignorant of the stage and its ways : hence the frequent
loss of temper on the part of those who *did* know the
requirements of dramatic art.

I shall never forget the effect on everybody when
Lady Martin was on the stage. No one dare speak to
her ; she went through the work as though she were
actually playing the part. We stood spell-bound before
her dignity, her splendid presence, her musical voice,
and rhythmetical utterance of blank verse—nay, more.
we applauded vigorously ; poor Wingfield was be-
witched and forgot his words, and as far as our own
individual work was concerned, we were demoralised.

After three months of worry and anxiety, the night of the 1st October arrived. Alfred Cellier took his seat in the orchestra, amidst a reception that showed how he was valued and respected by his Manchester friends. The Shakespearean overture was played, and then the "Address" was spoken. This address was written by Mr. H. M. Acton, so long honourably associated with the *Manchester Guardian*, and an old friend of Calvert's :—

ADDRESS.

Written by Mr. H. M. ACTON.

Stalls, pit, and gallery thronged, above, below!
What kindling motive prompts this glittering show?
Small need to ask—the sympathetic eye
And saddened smile are quick to make reply.
Beneath this roof, where, many a time, in quest
Of mirthful pastime, eager feet have pressed—
Where you and pleasure have so often met—
You come to-night to pay a generous debt;
To honour one now lowly laid, who bore
The Master's part in those glad scenes of yore.
He ruled this mimic kingdom, and how well
He swayed its sceptre none like *you* can tell.
The actor's calling—arduous at the best—
Hard school for vanity, and foe to rest—
Knows nothing worse, in all its list of ills,
Than when the sense of disappointment chills.
Who counts what aids of Heaven and Art unite
To form the whole that yields an hour's delight?
What careful pains and studious toil prepare
Effects which charm with seeming want of care?

Fame's own reward! but Fame's inconstant gale
Not always swells the most deserving sail!
With varying tastes, the treacherous standard shifts,
And Merit droops where praise crowns meaner gifts—
So frail our trust!   But none who Calvert knew
Will doubt his place among the foremost few,
Endowed by Nature, in a liberal hour,
With no small share of the great actor's power.
To every rendered phase of life he brought
Rich stores of cultured taste and earnest thought;
So nothing that he touched seemed tame or dim.
And Shakespeare's self spoke worthily through him.
True to the art he loved, whoe'er might fail,
He served her altar, though its fire grew pale.
Nor think that, when the actor's meed is paid,
Large e'en as he deserved, the whole is said.
Turn next where kindred hearts their grace combine
To bid Illusion's perfect triumph shine :
The glowing canvas, the voluptuous light,
The long-drawn pomp, the group that speaks at sight;
The self-same garb his living heroes wore,
And all their harness mocked with loving lore.
On themes like these bestowed, his ardent zeal
Made scenes, but half conceived before, seem real :
Arden's green glades, Miranda's island-home,
The martial grandeur of Imperial Rome,
The quays of Venice, Wolsey's princely halls,
Dover's white cliffs, and Harfleur's peopled walls;
All these arise, till, every access gained,
The captive senses scarce believe them feigned.
In vivid truth the poet's past returns;
In actual fire Sardanapalus burns;
And, fashioned as he lived, in sword and shield,
Our English Harry leads his troops a-field!
His claims were these : and if a thought arise

Of feelings based on nearer, homelier ties ;
Of her, companion of his struggling days,
Who shared their labour and partook the praise ;
Of children whom this hour may spur to fame,
Proud of the pride that decked their father's name ;
Reflect that where the deadliest blow was dealt,
You helped to make the pang less keenly felt ;
That while you paid to public worth its due,
A mourning hearth found faithful friends in you ;
And think with pleasure 'twas your hands that gave
A wreath of laurel to your favourite's grave.

After the applause which greeted the conclusion of the Address had subsided, the curtain rose, discovering Tom Taylor as Adam, and the Hon. Lewis Wingfield as Orlando. From the reception accorded to these two distinguished men, it was evident that the event was to be received with enthusiasm. It may at this point be desirable to insert a copy of the *final* programme. The only variation in it was caused by Linley Sambourne failing us at the last moment. Tom Taylor, who I believe was ready to fill every part in the piece, "doubled" Sambourne's part of Corin with his own fine impersonation of old Adam.

PROGRAMME.

The address, written by H. M. ACTON, Esq., will be spoken by
MRS. JOHN DUFFIELD,
Who has kindly undertaken the duty in the absence of
THE HON. LADY SEBRIGHT.

———

SHAKESPEARE'S COMEDY
"AS YOU LIKE IT."

From a Photograph by Lafosse, Manchester.

ALFRED DARBYSHIRE

AS "JAQUES" IN THE CALVERT MEMORIAL PERFORMANCE.

Dramatis Personae.

Duke (living in exile)		B. Lee, Esq.
Duke Frederick {Brother to the Duke, and Usurper of his Dominions}		Henry J. Jennings, Esq. (*Birmingham*)

First Lord . .
Second Lord . .
Third Lord . .   Lords attending
Fourth Lord . .   upon the Duke
Fifth Lord . .   in his
Amiens (with Songs)   Banishment
Jaques . . .

J. D. Watson, Esq., S.P.W.C.
. John Hollingshead, Esq.
. . G. du Maurier, Esq.
. . R. Watson, Esq.
. . W. Calder, Esq.
. Arthur Matthison, Esq.
A. Darbyshire, Esq., F.I.B.A.

Le Beau		C. Napier Hemy, Esq.
Charles (the Wrestler) . . .		R. J. Davies-Colley, Esq.
Oliver . . . Sons of {	. .	A. H. Marsh, Esq.
Jaques . . . Sir Rowland	. .	W. G. Baxter, Esq.
Orlando . . . de Bois. {	.	Hon. Lewis Wingfield.
Adam		. Tom Taylor, Esq.
Touchstone		Herman Merivale, Esq.
Corin . . . } Shepherds. {	.	Linley Sambourne, Esq.
Sylvius . . . }	. .	Arthur Poole, Esq.
William		. John Cavanah, Esq.
First Forester		. Edwin Waugh, Esq.
Rosalind (*Wednesday, October 1st*) . . .		Miss Wallis.
Rosalind (*Thursday, October 2nd*) {	Miss Helen Faucit, (*Mrs. Theodore Martin, now Lady Martin*).	
Celia . . . {	Miss Kate Pattison (*By kind permission of Messrs. Hare and Kendal*).	
Phebe		Miss Emma Toms (*Theatre Royal*).
Audrey		. Mrs. Edward Saker.

Stage Manager - MR. E. EDMONDS.

Chorus—Messrs. Downs, Fildes, Boardman, Fairhurst, Fawley, Becket, Allen, Wolstencroft, Broomhall, Kenyon, Page, Smethhurst, Muddiman, Lees, Law, Ruddock, Higson, Hart, Foulkes, Lynch, Dixon, Ray, Walton, Openshaw, Williamson.

Ladies of the Court and Shepherdesses—Mrs. Juliet Smith, Mrs. Thorpe, Miss Dow, Miss Harlow, Miss Richie, Miss Catterall, Miss Lynch, Mrs. Lynch.

Mr. Yardwood, Chorus Master.

Lords Attending upon Duke Frederick—Walter Lees, D. Anderson, F. Elkington, W. Humphreys, R. S. Nadin, H. Pagden, R. Daniels.

Foresters—W. Adams, A. Marriott, W. H. Rumsey, W. H. Meakin, A. T. Forrest, T. Cavanah, J. W. McGowan, J. Marriott, R. Winstanley, D. A. Murray, J. Harwood, J. Roberts, R. Pollitt, J. H. E. Partington, Charles Potter, H. Watkinson, W. Meredith.

MUSIC.

Shakespearean Overture	. . . . .	Sir. H. Bishop.
The Lorenzo Masque	Specially composed for the Revival of the Merchant of Venice.	Arthur Sullivan.
Pageant Music .	Specially composed for the Revival of Henry VIII.	Arthur Sullivan.
Revel Music .	Specially composed for the Revival of Sardanapalus.	Frederick Clay.

Musical Director   -   Mr. J. Crook.

Machinist—Mr. John Byrnes. | Gas Engineer—Mr. J. Watmouth.

Conductor of the Orchestra :

Mr. Alfred Cellier.

The Theatre placed at the disposal of the Committee by the Lessees— Messrs. Duffield and Lawton.

SCENE.

First near Oliver's House ; afterwards partly in the Usurper's Court and in the Forest of Arden.

THE MEMORIAL PROGRAMME

has been specially designed by

H. Stacy Marks, Esq,, R.A.

And the Original Drawing presented by him to the Committee.

Much has been written on these two performances of "As You Like it," and some of the distinguished men who played therein received well-merited commendation; but it was the presence of Helen Faucit which placed the cope-stone on the undertaking.

When she appeared on the stage, leaning on the arm of Celia (Miss Kate Pattison), the house rose *en masse*, and both from before and behind the curtain came a thunderclap of applause. For a few moments the great actress seemed stunned, but in a short time that beautiful voice rang through the theatre, and the play proceeded on its amateur career.

A volume might easily be written on the history of these eventful evenings, for the worries, troubles, and disappointments incident to the production of a piece by distinguished amateurs were only known to those who had the responsibility of carrying the event through to a successful issue. The crowded audiences who witnessed those two performances of "As You Like It" had no idea of the confusion and anxiety caused by the presence of two Rosalinds in the field. Each, of course, had different ideas of the character and its "business," and the consequence was that several of the actors got mixed, some forgetting in their excitement whether it was the Wallis night or the Faucit night. Even the poor little prompter got muddled; Louis Wingfield became so fascinated with the Faucit acting that he forgot to go on to his cue; dear Edwin Waugh, the beloved poet of Lancashire, who played the First Forester, forgot his entrance; and Arthur Matheson (the Amiens) had to say it was *he* who killed the deer, to avoid a stage wait.

We were inspired by Faucit's genius, and applauded at rehearsals. During the performance she startled me by the proposition to play the scene between Jaques and Rosalind, which, being "cut," we had not rehearsed in the morning. I agreed, and in a half-dazed, dream-like condition followed her on. I think as I went through it, we two, alone on the stage, it seemed to me the proudest moment of my life. There I stood with the "Goddess of my idolatry," the grand and noble woman, the finest actress of Shakespearean heroines since the days of Sarah Siddons.

The wonder now to me is, that I was not completely dazed with the glamour of the situation; but, somehow, the great genius of the woman carried me along like a torrent. I saw no audience, I heard nothing but the immortal words she had to speak. The dead silence at the "wings" and in the densely packed auditorium, haunts me to this day.

The curtain descended on another scene of enthusiasm, and for the *last time* hid from public view the commanding figure and the genius of Helen Faucit.

Helen Faucit was a stately lady, but withal a tender and good-hearted woman. She seemed when at work in great earnest, rehearsed as she intended to play, and thus compelled the respect of her brothers and sisters in art. She had a high appreciation for the Keane and Calvert methods of Shakespearean production, and made special journeys to Manchester to witness the Revivals at the Prince's Theatre. I well remember she expressed regret that it was impossible to impart to the "As You Like It" performances a "Revival" aspect. As one who took a small part in the Calvert Revivals, and defended the methods adopted, it was pleasant to have the high appreciation of such a cultured woman, and so great an artiste, as Helen Faucit.

Standing at the grave side, on a November morning in 1898, and taking a last look at Queen Victoria's wreath on her breast, the image of "heavenly Rosalind" rose before me as she was when she rendered the performance of "As You Like It" historic and memorable in the annals of the Manchester Stage.

The humours of the Calvert Memorial Performances were admirably dealt with in a magazine article by the late Herman Merivale (The Touchstone of the Event); but other points of interest may be briefly alluded to, and I will again quote from my book of "Experiences."

The dressing of the piece was a matter of much interest and discussion. Most of the men who had the principal characters allotted to them had hirsute appendages which they would not cut off—no, not even for Shakespeare! My suggestion was adopted that we should dress in what may be called the Holbein style; we, therefore, adopted the English Renaissance costume of the time of Henry VIII., and the result was eminently satisfactory and picturesque. We had, however, to run the gauntlet of the sketcher and the newspaper illustrator. Both on and off the stage we could hardly turn round, without seeing a crowd of these gentlemen busy at work; they followed one about, and even confronted their subjects with, "One moment, sir"; "Thanks—that will do," etc. J. D. Watson, with that enthusiasm which characterised his actions when

picturesque costume was in the ascendant, actually put
on an Inverness cloak and coolly went into the stalls to
draw Rosalind. We may be thankful for this eccentric
action, for it gave to the *Graphic* an excellent full-
length portrait of Helen Faucit, the last taken of her
in stage attire and in the character of that immortal
heroine she loved so well. I take some pride in the
recollection that the Calvert Memorial Performances
were successful from an artistic point of view. We
were earnestly solicited to transfer the whole affair to
the Metropolis; but as one and all declared they would
not go without their goddess, Helen Faucit, the idea
was abandoned. That they were successful financially was, of course, the main cause for congratulation.
Everybody appeared *con amore*. There was nothing
to pay of any consequence. H. Stacy Marks, R.A.,
gave us his beautiful drawing for the back of the programme; this we sold for a large sum, which was
added to the proceeds. The amount realised was
little short of £1,000, which was placed in the hands
of trustees for the benefit of the dear ones left behind
by the man whose memory we all delighted to honour.

I have incorporated thus much of Calvert's career
in this book because it is now generally admitted that
his work was good, healthy, and noble in its aspirations;
and because what he did for the Stage in Manchester
affected the theatrical enterprise of the country; and
lastly—because I was so intimately associated with his
work and professionally connected with the little
building in which his noblest efforts were made.

Perhaps nothing better has been said of Calvert and his work than in the utterance of the late noble Bishop Fraser, at the Social Science Congress held in 1879. He said :—

In the present state of artistic and literary education, the taste of our people is so coarse and unrefined, that it is almost impossible to prevent their amusements from degrading into vulgarity and indecency. Mrs. Theodore Martin, with that generosity which is characteristic of her, is this very night performing in the Theatre Royal, as a mark of respect to the memory of the late Mr. Charles Calvert, who did so much, not in Manchester only, but in other provincial towns, to up· hold the character of the stage. I remember well on one occasion, when I endeavoured to show in public my approbation of his efforts— for which I am afraid I fell into the black books of many sincerely good, but gloomy people—that in acknowledging what I said, he told me what up-hill work he found it, and how constantly his aims were defeated by the vicious public taste, not only of the lower class— which preferred what was indelicate, and prurient, and revolting.

With the death of Charles Calvert, it may truly be said that the decay of the Manchester Stage commenced. The effort made by Calvert and his partner Browne was universally respected and encouraged, and a vast amount of prejudice against the Theatre was removed. After what I have quoted of Bishop Fraser's utterance at the Science Congress, it will readily be believed that I once heard him tell Calvert that the Theatre, in his hands, might run with the pulpit in its influence for good. The public utterances of the noble-hearted prelate in connection with theatrical amusements, always tended towards this fact. Manchester people who had been accustomed to the higher art of Charles Calvert, hurled back the "sacred lamp of burlesque," and sent its crestfallen advocates back to London, wiser but sadder men.

As long as the annals of our national Stage last, the name of Charles Alexander Calvert will appear as that of a man, actor, and manager who enhanced the value and upheld the honour of the art of the Victorian Stage.

CHAPTER V.

CALVERT'S SUCCESSORS IN MANCHESTER.

THE decadence of the Manchester Stage, after the removal of Charles Calvert, lasted many years; and the *prestige* obtained by the only provincial city of the Empire, for the maintenance of the highest art of the Stage in the latter half of the Victorian Era, seemed to the lovers of theatrical art, to be entirely lost. In the year 1896 an event occurred which has resulted in an extraordinary revival of the Shakespearean drama; and this event is owing to the courage of Richard Flanagan, the Lessee of the Queen's Theatre. Mr. Flanagan had the advantage of being one of Calvert's assistants at the Prince's Theatre during that wonderful decade of the art of the stage of which I have treated in the foregoing chapter. He was thoroughly imbued with the *raison d'être* of what had been achieved, and resolved to take the risk of running a theatre on the same lines. The result is now historic in the annals of the Stage.

I have sometimes thought that a parallel may be

drawn between the work of Phelps and Flanagan.
I have already written of the heroic work done by
Phelps in the little Islington theatre away from the
centre of metropolitan culture, and although the Queen's
Theatre in Manchester is not so far removed from the
theatrical centre as was Sadler's Wells, it possessed no
particular *prestige* until Richard Flanagan took possession and inaugurated the run of the Shakespearean
drama in January, 1896. Whatever criticism and whatever fault may be found with the detail of the great
work of the last ten years, the thanks of lovers of high
dramatic art are due to the man who has had the
courage and determination to produce high-class work
in a second-rate theatre and at popular prices. It stands
to reason that under such conditions the histrionic part
of the work had to be secured at prices which could
scarcely command the highest acting art; everything
has been beautifully and thoughtfully carried out. In
the mounting of the revivals of the Shakespearean
drama Mr. Flanagan has been blamed for introducing
scene and spectacle not forming part of the plays.
Charles Calvert incurred rather severe criticism for
introducing that splendid tableaux of the Battle of
Agincourt; so also did Sir Henry Irving for the last
scene of " Ravenswood." I have looked upon such
fault-finding as indicating a want of sufficient thought
as to the object and meaning of such illustrations.
They give point and accentuate the value of the poet's
meaning, and are perfectly legitimate so long as they
are done in silence and no words are introduced beyond

what the author has set down for utterance.   They are
also of educational value, as in the instance of the
Agincourt Tableau alluded to, which was a complete,
perfect, and artistic exposition ; in fact a living
military picture of the early years of the fifteenth
century.

It is interesting to note that Flanagan's first Shakespearean production of " Henry IV.," in 1896, was the
result of the knowledge and superintendence of Louis
Calvert, the worthy son of a worthy sire, and whose
mother curiously enough played Dame Quickly.   The
revival of this seldom enacted play ran for four weeks.
The Manchester Guardian wrote in a leading article :
" Manchester playgoers will flock to hear the great
dramas performed by an intelligent company, at popular
prices, just as readily as they did twenty years ago."
Although Louis Calvert's talents as a play mounter
have been transferred to London, Flanagan has continued his Shakesperean revivals yearly since 1896, and
the Queen's Theatre, in Manchester, is the only home
out of the Metropolis for what we are pleased to call
Shakespearean "revivals."   Flanagan's work has proved
an interesting fact, namely, that hard working men and
women of a great manufacturing centre will stand by
and support the manager who will produce the works
of our great dramatist in a worthy, intelligent, and
illustrative manner.   As Richard Flanagan may take
his place with those who have contributed towards the
maintenance of the highest art of the Victorian Stage,
I will here place on record the " Queen's " Revivals in

order of date, with the number of performances of each play.

Henry IV. . . .	28	performances
Antony and Cleopatra .	55	,,
Macbeth·. . . .	57	,,
Winter's Tale . . .	58	,,
Much Ado about Nothing	84	,,
Merchant of Venice. .	112	,,
Merry Wives of Windsor	77	,,
Henry VIII. . . .	78	,,
Richard III. . . .	85	,,
Romeo and Juliet . .	106	,,

Cymbeline ran for fourteen weeks.

"Cymbeline" was played to crowded houses ; it was beautifully mounted and highly appreciated. I wish the scope of this work would allow of detailed mention of the artists, and their work, who have assisted Flanagan in his annual productions, but it does not. I must only record that the pictorial beauties of the productions at the Queen's Theatre are, and have been, the work of the scenic artists, Palmer and Freemantle. The architecture has been worked out with great knowledge and research by the former ; and to the latter great credit is due for beautiful landscape work and picturesque architectural adjuncts.

Although this is intended as a record of the art of the Victorian Stage, it is impossible to ignore the work of Robert Courtneidge which was inaugurated at the Prince's Theatre, Manchester, in the first year of Edward

VII. The Courtneidge "Revivals" consisted of the two comedies, "A Midsummer Night's Dream" and "As You Like It," and were the result of that stage art generated and maintained in the Era of which I am writing, and may be considered as the wind-up of Shakesperean production of the Victorian Stage. It would be impossible, except at considerable length, to give a fair and detailed record of these two beautiful art productions of the Stage of our time. To those who believe in giving pictorial expression to the works of the greatest dramatist the world has known, the sight of these two exquisite productions was delightful; they were regarded with thankfulness, inasmuch as they represented what the poet had in his mind when he wrote the plays, and what he would have done with them had the Stage of his time been equal to such a method of representation. I shall always remember being present with Ellen Terry and Sir Henry Irving at a morning performance of these two immortal comedies. We were curiously affected, giving way to tears, sighs, and thankfulness. I have already quoted what my dear old friend said on the fall of the curtain on "As You Like It," and I am bound to confess that I am thankful I have lived to see such a pictorial and histrionic representation of the queen of comedies. It is only fair to admit that what is called the "new school" of acting seemed to suit the work in a marvellous manner. I remember Irving saying to me, "If these people are right, how terribly wrong we must have been; who ever heard of or saw Jacques on a rustic stool at a table, from which he gave the seven age speech, and never rose from it, not even on the delivery of the final line, and yet the house rose to the situation." I reminded Sir Henry that this new school had been really grounded by himself, and that he gave the "To be or not to be" speech from an arm chair. Such is the acting which goes with the art of the Stage, generated in the latter half of the Victorian Era, and which succeeded that formed on conventional and academic principles.

Robert Courneidge, alas! left the theatrical world of Manchester after the production of these two exquisite works of stage art; but I have placed in the appendix copies of the cast, and the names of the musicians and painters in order that a permanent record may be kept of what I consider two historic events in the art and modern development of the English Stage.

In 1903 Courtneidge took these two productions to Australia. On his departure the citizens of Manchester wished him *bon voyage* at a public gathering in the Prince's Theatre. An address was presented and deposited in a beautiful silver casket specially designed in the Elizabethan style of ornament. The success of the "Midsummer Night's Dream" and "As You Like It" in Australia was phenomenal. He wrote me from Melbourne on the production of the former play; in his letter, dated April 20th, 1903, he writes: "There is no doubt that we are in for a boom, and that in spite of the fact that the croaker was well in evidence before we opened, just in the old sweet fashion. The letters from schools are pouring in, and I expect to see the children, as in Manchester, having their first impression of the Stage from the highest and best." In another letter he writes: "As You Like It" is playing to magnificent houses." The wish to see the plays was extraordinary and, according to the Melbourne press, hundreds were nightly turned away. Such success is a proof that the masses of English-speaking people will support the highest kind of drama mounted in the method perfected in the Victorian period of Stage art, and the name of Robert Courtneidge will ever be treasured in its annals.

The playgoers of Manchester may well take a pride in the fact that they have supported the managers who have devoted their best energies and their money to the representation of the best and highest art of the Stage.

CHAPTER VI.

SIR HENRY IRVING.

I AM conscious that in placing the name of the foremost actor-manager of his time at the head of this chapter I have imposed upon myself a task of great importance and very difficult of fulfilment. The difficulty is increased by the fact that I enjoyed his friendship from youthful days, and the temptation is strong to indulge in details which do not affect the object of my work, which is to chronicle the achievements of the late great actor-manager and their extraordinary effect on the Stage art of the Victorian Era.

It is a curious thing that the theatre of Manchester should again be associated with a great historical epoch in the development of the art of the Victorian Stage. It was in that city that Henry Irving seriously entered on his life of histrionic art, and it is desirable that a short record should be given of his work in Manchester and in the County of Lancaster.

From a Somerset cottage to Westminster Abbey! There is no phase of human life more interesting to study than that which begins in humbleness and ends in glory. Such life has produced and will produce an influence which bears materially on the history and *prestige* of a nation. A great American President, Abraham Lincoln, commenced life in a log cabin and ended in the White House. The period of this transit was fraught with importance and value and has resulted in increased civilisation and freedom to mankind. This kind of life has been known in the political world, both ancient and modern, but in the art world of the Theatre the career of Sir Henry Irving is unique, and I sometimes wonder whether his countrymen have fully realized the magnitude of his work in the art of and for the Theatre as an institution. The effect of Irving's work on the present generation has been extraordinary, the prejudice against the Theatre has been entirely removed; the Lyceum, from the memorable night of its opening, December 30th, 1878, and as long as it was under the control of Irving, was the rallying place of all classes of society and the common ground of culture, refinement, and art. I know of nothing in the history of modern civilisation that can compare with the revolution in thought and idea caused by Irving's work in connection with the Theatre as a national institution. When we think of the past history and vicissitudes of the drama in this country we are able to realize what has been achieved; when we think that this change was mainly owing to Henry Irving we are not surprised that a gracious Queen expressed her pleasure (as some of us know she did) when Sir Henry rose from his kneeling position with the honour of knighthood. When we reflect that a grateful people saw his remains consigned to the grandest and most poetic resting place a nation can offer, then the conviction is forced upon us that a man of humble origin has achieved a great work, and which has been fully acknowledged by grateful country-men and loving friends.

Although it is not my intention in this work to detail the events and vicissitudes of Irving's early life, it seems desirable that the first important period in his career should receive some attention in these pages. There can be no doubt that Irving's ultimate method of stage work was the result of his few years' life in Man-chester, and his association with Charles Calvert, who was the manager for Knowles at the Theatre Royal.

It may be well to note, for the information of the present generation, that it was the custom to have the theatres worked by what was called a Stock Company, and it was in September, 1860, after severe experience in Sunderland, Edinburgh, and other towns, as a member of the Theatre Royal Stock Company, the young actor, Henry Irving, made his first bow to a Manchester audience in a piece called " The Spy, or a Government Appointment." Much has been said and written of a certain ungainliness of deportment and a peculiarity of pronunciation which characterised the early work of Irving as an actor. I well remember watching a rehearsal at the Theatre Royal, when some-one came up to Calvert and asked the question, "Why on earth did you engage that raw fellow?" (pointing to Irving). Calvert replied by touching his forehead with his forefinger, and indicated that what he had engaged him for lay in the brain. Curiously enough, in after years, dear Johnny Toole, as we used to call him, told me that when Charles Dickens saw "Uncle Dick's Darling," with Irving as Chevenix, it was a revelation to him, and he prophesied a brilliant future for the young actor. How keenly the great novelist could read and create character; how far this prophecy has been fulfilled, all the world knows.

Irving's life in Manchester, both socially and professionally, was pleasantly spent. After his accession to the stock company of the Royal, Calvert took an immediate interest in the young recruit, and a friendship resulted between them of which many interesting anecdotes might be told. It is to me an interesting fact that I should have my introduction to Irving through my friend Calvert, and that between the two men I have enjoyed two of the most cherished friendships of my life.

It was not long before Henry Irving won his way to the hearts of Lancashire audiences, and when he said farewell to them in 1865 the event was marked by much enthusiasm. I was elected a member of a committee, constituted for the purpose of organising a series of farewell benefits, and to speed the departing actor on his London career, under the auspices of the late Dion Boucicault, at the St. James's Theatre. The first benefit performance took place at the Free Trade Hall,

Manchester. This event was of such importance that I shall here insert the programme :—

FREE TRADE HALL.—Wed., April 12, 1865.

Mr. HENRY IRVING'S

FAREWELL BENEFIT.

The following ladies and gentlemen have kindly volunteered their Services (by permission of Mr. Charles Calvert) :—

Miss Alice Dodd.
Miss Florence Haydon.
Miss Maud Haydon.
Mr. Frederick Maccabe.
Mr. Philip Day.

Assisted by Captain Lathbury, together with Messrs. John Cavanah and W. Ellis, of the Manchester Athenæum Literary and Dramatic Society; and Mr. E. Howard of the De Trafford Club.

An Address, written by Fox Turner, Esq., will be delivered by Mr. Henry Irving.

The Performance will commence with the COMEDIETTA of
"WHO SPEAKS FIRST?"

Mr. Maccabe will appear in a selection from his popular entertainment, "Begone Dull Care," and will recite (in character) the poem of "Shamus O'Brien."

SONG   -   -   "Home, Sweet Home" - Miss Alice Dodd.

THE MYSTERY OF
THE CABINET AND DARK SEANCE
(à la Davenport)

Will be explained and produced without the aid of darkness by Messrs. Maccabe and Day, assisted by Mr. Irving as the Doctor.

To conclude with the FARCE of
"RAISING THE WIND."

Mr. McQuade will conduct the Band of the 64th Regiment.

The exposure of the tricks of the Davenport Brothers was a triumph ; and Mr. Irving's imitation of Doctor Fergusson was a magnificent piece of satire. Speaking of this portion of the performance, the *Manchester Guardian* said : " The hall was crowded with an enthusiastic audience. The whole of the tricks were speedily accomplished, and the exposure was most complete and satisfactory to the audience, who made the hall ring alternately with laughter and applause."

The inhabitants of Bury (an important town near Manchester) were anxious to have a share in these farewell performances, and a committee was formed for carrying out this object. This event will always dwell vividly in my memory, inasmuch as I had the pleasure of playing in both the tragedy and the farce. When I look back to those far-off days, it seems almost a dream, and I can scarcely realise the fact that I once "trod the boards" with the man, who was my friend, and the first actor ever honoured with a title by the Sovereign of these realms.

This performance in the town of Bury was Irving's final farewell to Lancashire as a stock actor. I shall always remember this event because I had to enact the part of Polonius, in a King Lear robe lent me by Charles Calvert. The success of this experimental performance of Hamlet was such that it had to be repeated a second time, and concluded in an overwhelming burst of farewell enthusiasm. I consider this event an important item in the life and work of Sir Henry Irving, and therefore I reproduce the play bill.

AMATEUR DRAMATIC PERFORMANCE,

Athenæum, Bury.

FOR ONE NIGHT ONLY.

Friday, June 23rd, 1865.

SHAKESPEARE'S TRAGEDY OF

"H A M L E T,"

With New Scenery, Painted expressly for the occasion by
Messrs. F. W. Livesey and T. Shaw.

To conclude with an Exposure and Explanation of the so-called
Spiritualism of the

DAVENPORT BROTHERS,

As recently given by Messrs. Irving, Maccabe, and Day, at the
Free Trade Hall, Manchester.

HAMLET.

Hamlet	Mr. Henry Irving (*Late of the Theatre Royal, Manchester*).
The Ghost	Mr. B. Lee.
Claudius	
Horatio	
Rosencrantz	
Osric	
Marcellus	
Bernardo	By Gentlemen Amateurs of Bury.
Francisco	
Guildenstern	
First Player	
Second Player	
Second Gravedigger	
Priest	
Polonius	
Laertes	By Gentlemen Amateurs of Manchester.
First Gravedigger	
The Queen	Miss Reinhardt (*From the Prince's Theatre, Manchester*).
Ophelia	Miss Florence Haydon (*From the Prince's Theatre Manchester*).
First Actress	Miss Maud Haydon (*From the Prince's Theatre, Manchester*).

Exposure and Explanation of the so-called Spiritualism
of the
DAVENPORT BROTHERS.

Dr. Fergusson . . . . Mr. Henry Irving.
Musical Director . · . . . John M. Wike, Esq.

No Money will be taken at the Doors.

Admission by Tickets only, which may be obtained from Mr. Crompton, Bookseller, Fleet Street ; and Mr. W. S. Barlow, Bookseller, Haymarket Street.

Private Boxes, £1 10s. ; Boxes, 2s. 6d. ; Pit, 1s. ;
Gallery, 6d.

A few Stall Tickets, numbered and reserved, price 5s. each, may be had at Mr. Crompton's, where a Plan of the Seats may be seen.

Doors open at Seven o'clock; Performance to commence at half-past.

Irving thoroughly enjoyed this initial performance of the great tragedy. I recollect he filled both his fellow-actors and his audience with enthusiasm. Although we were all impressed with the actor's rendering of Hamlet, little did we dream that in after-years our Prince of Denmark was to take the world by storm by an accentuated and matured rendering of the psychology of the part.

For some reason, which I have forgotten, the Davenport business did not come off, and a farce, " My Wife's Dentist," was put up at a moment's notice. I remember Irving played the title-rôle, and Lee and myself the other two male characters. Shall I ever forget that farce ? Neither of us "got the words," and the nonsense we talked was so dreadful that Irving frequently dashed on the stage and very adroitly got us off, amidst the uproarious laughter of the audience.

Some curious incidents happened. I recollect I played Polonius (wearing a beard which I would *not* cut off); it was thought that my flowing fur-trimmed robe would go well with the hirsute appendage. My arms were bare, and altogether I must have looked very barbaric. Amateur-like, I burst out laughing when Irving said in a very pointed manner, and a merry twinkle in his eye, "*You* to the barber's with your beard." I remember the weather was very hot, and after being consigned to oblivion, I was sitting on a table behind the tapestry, fanning myself, when, to my astonishment, Hamlet drew aside the tapestry, and repeating the well-known words, "Thou rash, intruding fool, I took thee for thy betters," he gave me an agonised look, and *sotto voce* exclaimed: "For goodness' sake get me a pint of stout! I'm as dry as a limekiln." This, from the Prince of Denmark, startled me, and for some little time I failed to take in the situation.

It is curious to note the effect of acting a great part like Hamlet upon different temperaments. Sir Henry Irving threw his whole soul into such an impersonation, and the thirsty anecdote I have just told reminds me that once if not twice during the play a complete change of garments was necessary, when he was enacting this trying part. I once asked Barry Sullivan how the part affected him physically. He replied, in that peculiar tone of voice, and tragic action, we so well remember, "Never turn a hair, sir!" Many years after the performance of "Hamlet" at Bury, the two tragedians, Irving and Sullivan, happened to be playing in

Manchester at the same time, Sullivan at the Queen's, Irving at the Royal ; and curiously enough, "Hamlet" was in the Bill at both theatres.   I do not think a greater contrast could be possible, than between the one actor, who was all soul and intellect, and the other, "who never turned a hair, sir," and who was conventional and histrionically academic.   The most curious sight I ever saw in connection with dramatic history in my time, was that of Irving and Sullivan sitting side by side at a dinner; Sullivan being Irving's guest.   A distinguished gathering witnessed this strange juxta-position of two theatrical stars ; and one felt that the last link was about to be broken between the traditions of the "high and palmy" school, and that of the original and cultured body of actors who are forming the histrionic art of the 20th century.   Barry Sullivan, the last of his race, was soon to depart to "that bourn from whence no traveller returns;" alas! Sir Henry Irving has followed him, and the world has lost a great and good man.

It is a curious fact that the man or woman of genius is never afraid of looking back upon the days of small things.   Early struggles amid humble surroundings are regarded from the high standpoint of success as pleasant memories ; and Sir Henry Irving was no exception in this respect.   I know that this performance of "Hamlet" in the Lancashire town was remembered with pleasure by the great actor and manager, and I therefore have no hesitation in recording incidents of an event which is historic in his career, and which is a pleasant memory to myself.

In the year 1881, on the 23rd of September, Sir Henry Irving was entertained at a Banquet, given in his honour, at the Queen's Hotel, Manchester.* Professor Ward was in the chair. Sir Henry's speech, in reply to the toast of his health, was characteristic of the man, and as it substantiates what I have written as to the pleasure the great man took in looking back on his early and struggling life, I will conclude my reference to his Manchester experiences by quoting it from the press of the time. Sir Henry said :—

"I lived here for five years, and wherever I look—to the right or to the left, to the north or to the south—I always find some remembrance, some memento of those five years—youthful aspirations, youthful hopes, battles fought, battles won, battles lost, early ambitions, and many things that fill my mind with pleasure and sometimes with pain. But there is one association connected with my life that probably is unknown to but a few in this room. That is an association with a friend, which had much to do, I believe, with the future course of our two lives. When I tell you that our communions were very grave and very deep, that our friendship was a strong one, and for months and years we fought together, and worked together to the best of our power, and with the means we had then, to give effect to the art we were practicing; when I tell you we dreamt of what might be done, but was not done, and patted each other on the back and said, 'Well, old fellow, perhaps the day will come when you may have a little more than sixpence in your pocket;' when I tell you that that man was well-known to you, and that his name was Calvert, you will understand the nature of my associations with Manchester. Our lives were separated even while he lived, and our intercourse ceased altogether; he was working here

---

* For this event I designed the menu card, which was a pictorial reference to the work done at the Lyceum and to Sir Henry's association with Shakespearean Revival.

and I was working elsewhere. I have no doubt you will be able to trace in my own career, and the success I have had, the benefit of the communion I had with him. When I was in Manchester I had very many friends. I needed good advice at that time, for I found it a very difficult thing as an actor to pursue my profession, and to do justice to certain things that I always had a deep, and perhaps rather an extravagant, idea of, on the sum of £75 a year. I have been making a calculation within the last few minutes of the amount of money that I did earn in those days, and I found it was about £75 a year. Perhaps one would be acting out of the fifty-two weeks of the year some thirty-five. The other part of the year one would probably be receiving nothing. Then an actor would be tempted perhaps to take a benefit, by which he generally lost £20 or £30. Any friends of mine present who may have thought a little less of me at that time, perhaps because of my continuous state of impecuniosity, will forgive me when I confess the amount of my earnings. However, that time is past, but if there are any odd half-crowns that I owe I shall be glad to pay them. I have a very fond recollection, I have an affection for your city, for very many reasons. The training I received here, which Professor Ward has alluded to, was a severe training; I must say at first it was very severe. I found it a difficult thing to make my way at all with the audience; and I believe the audience, to a certain extent, was right; I think there was no reason that I should make my way with them. I don't think I had learnt enough; I think I was too raw, too unacceptable. But I am very proud to say that it was not long before, with the firmness of the Manchester friendship which I have always found, they got to like me; and I think before I parted with them they had an affection for me. At all events, I remember when in this city as little less—or little more—than a walking gentleman, I essayed the part of Hamlet, the Dane, I was looked upon as a sort of madman, who ought to be taken to a sort of asylum and shut up; but I found in acting it before the audience that their opinion was a very different one, and before the play was half gone through I was received with a fervour and a kindness which gave me hope and expectation that in the far and distant future I might perhaps be able to benefit by their kindness. If they had not treated me so, if they had chilled me, probably they would have done so, little knowing how sometimes such a reception may change the life and the career of an artist. Perhaps they thought that by encouraging me they might help me on in the future. I believe they thought that, I believe that was in the thoughts of many of the audience, for they received me with an enthusiasm and kindness which my merits did not deserve."

After leaving Lancashire for London, Irving's life and career may be divided into three distinct epochs: the first epoch will embrace the engagements at various London theatres, the second period will comprise his Lyceum experiences under the Bateman and his own management, and the third may date from the end of the Lyceum *régime* to the close of his life.

The first epoch I have mentioned can only receive brief notice, as Irving's influence over the art of the Victorian Stage really commenced when he was finally fixed at the Lyceum. It is essential, however, that some allusion should be made to those years in London, during which he attracted notice as an actor. Boucicault engaged him to play in his piece, "The Two Lives of Mary Leigh," and I recollect seeing the Company at a Manchester Theatre; and on which occasion I first saw Ellen Terry, whose sister Kate was in the piece. This was in the year after Irving left Lancashire, and some time in 1866. The play was done in London under the new title of "Hunted Down," and in which Irving may be said to have made his first important success in the character of Rawdon Scudamore. The play was acted at the St. James's Theatre with great success, with my old friend, Ada Dyas, as the suffering wife. The success of this play quite prepared us for the next success in "Uncle Dick's Darling," when Irving played Chevenix for his dear friend, J. L. Toole. I have already quoted the opinion of Charles Dickens on the creation and performance of this character. Byron's play was always welcomed wherever it went, and Irving scored another acting success.

I trust there are still living persons who remember that exquisite and fascinating play of "The Two Roses." This was impersonated by a highly-gifted and lovable company of men and women. In addition to Henry Irving I remember H. J. Montague, George Honey, and Amy Fawcitt, all, alas! now removed from the roll of theatrical fame. It may be reasonably concluded that in the character of Digby Grant, Irving settled beyond doubt his claim to be one of the best actors of the period.

It is not to be wondered at that a manager, launching on theatrical venture, should desire to secure the services and co-operation of an actor who was so highly appreciated by a London play-going public as Henry Irving; accordingly we find that when Bateman (or the "Colonel" as we used to call him) became the lessee of the historic Lyceum Theatre, he secured Irving as the main prop of his theatrical venture. I may here inform my readers, or those who are not already aware of the fact, that Bateman was the father of Miss Bateman (Mrs. Crowe) who became famous in the play

of "Leah," and of Isabel, who played the principal
women parts to Irving during the *régime* of her father
at the Lyceum. The Batemans came from America;
but English people who know anything of the Victorian
Theatre have ever held the family in high respect, and
fully appreciate the kindly feeling which existed between
the family and our great English actor, Sir Henry
Irving.

The Lyceum, under the Bateman management,
opened in 1871. I recollect the "Colonel" produced a
piece called "Fanchette," which was a failure. This
was followed by what may be considered a historic
success of Victorian Stage art. "The Bells" was
adapted from a French source by Lewis, and the
character of Mathias illustrated for the first time the
creative genius of Sir Henry Irving. This genius was
again displayed to an extraordinary extent in the play,
which succeeded "The Bells," written by Wills, and
known in the catalogue of original dramas as "Charles
I." Those persons who saw this supreme effort will
ever cherish a pleasant memory of the life-like portrait
of the unfortunate monarch. They will ever remember
the parting of the King from his family on leaving for
the scaffold. This was a triumph of histrionic art.

After these two original representations, the Bateman management, either under the "Colonel" or his
wife, produced "Hamlet," first performed October 31st,
1874, and which ran for two hundred performances;
"Macbeth" with eighty performances; "Othello" with
seventy representations; and "Richard III." with a run

of two hundred nights. I do not recollect any special features in these productions, but I remember Irving was subjected to much adverse and carping criticism on his interpretation of these great Shakespearean characters. When Bateman died in 1875, his widow took on the lease of the theatre, and in 1878 it became desirable that she should retire from the responsibility. Her retirement marked the greatest event in the history of the stage art of the Victorian Era, inasmuch as it gave Irving an opportunity of realising the desire of his heart, in the production of the high art of the Stage entirely on his own responsibility. In 1878 he took over the lease of the Lyceum, and so inaugurated the greatest era in the modern history of the Stage.

The year 1878 was one of great professional interest to me, inasmuch as my old friend, after becoming lessee of the Lyceum, consulted me as to the necessary alterations and decorations of the fabric. I should not allude to this matter here, but my professional association brought me into contact with many interesting and remarkable persons, and enabled me to fully understand the *raison d'être* of Irving's management. I was a partaker in many artistic and social events which are still to me pleasant memories.

I have alluded, at the commencement of this work, to the two great epochs of dramatic art being marked by the reigns of two great English Queens. It is a curious thing that the Lyceum Theatre stands on the site of the house occupied by Burleigh, the great minister of Queen Elizabeth and contemporary with the dramatist whose immortal works found the most magnificent expression by the great actor-manager of the reign of Queen Victoria.

I need not enter into the details of my work at the Lyceum Theatre, done for my friend and to the satisfaction of the Lord Chamberlain and Mr. Arnold the owner. Suffice it to say that the works were of much importance, and that nothing of historic art value was injured or destroyed. The Bartolozzi ornaments on the circle fronts were maintained with that respect due to the work of a great artist, who was the father of Madame Vestris, once the lessee of the theatre. I recollect on one occasion, during the carrying out of the decorative work, the venerable Walter Lacy was present when the ceiling of the auditorium was being stripped prior to the new scheme of decoration. The process revealed a scheme of ornament in imitation of lace work on a pink coloured ground. On showing a piece of this to the good old actor he exclaimed, "This is a portion of the work done to please Madame Vestris! Why! my boy, the whole place was hung with imitation lace ; it was a fairy-like oriental ecstacy! The figure groups and raised ornaments were modelled by Bartolozzi."

My work at the Lyceum opened up a delightful experience, especially a knowledge and acquaintance with Sir Henry Irving's good friend the Baroness Burdett-Coutts. This is a treatise on the art of the Victorian Stage, therefore I must abandon this digression. I shall never forget, however, the delightful times I spent in Stratton Street, Piccadilly, the people of importance in the art and literary world I met there, and the pleasant time I spent at Holly Lodge, Highgate, elaborating a scheme for its enlargement and improvement for my highly esteemed client the Baroness Burdett-Coutts.

The alterations and decorations to which I have referred were completed in time for the opening of the theatre on the last Saturday in 1878. With this opening the great work of theatre reform and dramatic production commenced, by which the memory of Irving will be carried along the coming ages.

There were many bright and original thoughts associated with the Irving *régime* at the Lyceum, but the most brilliant of all was the initial one of selecting an actress whose temperament and emotional art should run in parallel lines with the acting methods of the actor-manager. It was a supreme thought which resulted in the association of Ellen Terry and Henry Irving in the great work inaugurated at the Lyceum on the memorable night of the end of December, 1878.

Those who are still living, and who remember that opening night with the revival of "Hamlet," will understand my meaning as to the value of Ellen Terry, and her histrionic art, in conjunction with that of the man who was to become the greatest, and most honoured, actor of the Victorian Era. I think the scene of the renunciation of Hamlet's love for Ophelia realised the grandest episode of Shakespearean invention confined to a dual piece of histrionic art. The remembrance of this realisation will last "as long as memory holds her seat." The Shakespearean playgoer will recollect the point in the scene when Ophelia says :—

> "My Lord, I have remembrances of yours
> That I have longed long to re-deliver,
> I pray you now receive them."

From this point Irving gradually worked himself into a passion, during which he renounced his love for Ophelia ; the passion, however, subsided, weakness got the better of him, and in the last repetition of the exclamation, " Get thee to a Nunnery," he returned from the back of the stage, and almost placed his arms around the seated figure of Ophelia ; but with a painful effort he refrained. The beautiful face of Ophelia turned in astonishment, and with tear-bedewed eyes she gazed into Hamlet's face, and knew that he had loved her with a great and honest love. The exit of Hamlet was made in a silence that was profound, but on the exit of Ophelia, at the close of the beautiful speech which ends

> "Like sweet bells jangled, out of tune and harsh,
> O woe is me!
> To have seen what I have seen, see what I see,"

the pent-up emotions of that wonderful audience found vent in one of those unanimous shouts of applause which constitute the finest tribute to the histrionic artist. The audience left the theatre with an absolute conviction that Shakespeare intended Hamlet to love Ophelia truly and devotedly ; a love declared at her graveside which could not be exceeded by that of forty thousand brothers "who could not with all their quantity of love make up my sum." On this first night of

" Hamlet," in 1878, the house was packed from floor to ceiling, and contained the best of intellect and culture in the realms of literature and art. Such an audience admitted with acclamation such a triumph of histrionic art, and concluded that with a coalition of genius and temperament, as developed in the persons of Henry Irving and Ellen Terry, the future would produce great and historic results. Such results have accentuated the grandeur and the beauty of the art of the Victorian Stage.

The opening night of the Lyceum under Irving's own management was such an important event in the stage art of the period I am writing of, that I consider it desirable to reproduce the cast of " Hamlet" on that occasion.

Hamlet	Mr. Irving.
Claudius	Mr. Forrester.
Polonius	Mr. Chippendale.
Laertes	Mr. F. Cooper.
Horatio	Mr. Swinbourne.
Osric	Mr. Kyrle Bellew.
Rosencrantz	Mr. Pinero.
Guildenstern	Mr. Elwood.
Marcellus	Mr. Gibson.
Bernardo	Mr. Robinson.
Francisco	Mr. Tapping.
Reynaldo	Mr. Cartwright.
First Player	Mr. Beaumont.
Second Player	Mr. Everard.
Priest	Mr. Collett.
First Gravedigger	Mr. S. Johnson.
Second Gravedigger	Mr. A. Andrews.
Messenger	Mr. Harwood.
Ghost of Hamlet's Father	Mr. Mead.
Gertrude	Miss Pouncefort.
Player Queen	Miss Sedley.

and

Ophelia	Miss Ellen Terry.

Mr. Hawes Craven painted the scenery, and Mr. Hamilton Clarke was the Musical Director.

"Hamlet" was played one hundred and eight nights, and during that first season of seven months, the receipts amounted to £36,000.

It is quite impossible to include in this work a detailed account of Irving's productions at the Lyceum. Such an account would fill a volume, and until a life of the great actor is forthcoming, we must rest content with the effort made by my friend, Mr. Percy Fitzgerald, in his interesting volume entitled, "Twenty Years at the Lyceum." In order that an idea may be obtained of the magnitude and importance of Irving's *règime* at the Lyceum, a list of productions may here be introduced.

As before stated the Lyceum opened under Irving's management on the night of December 30th, 1878, with "Hamlet" which ran for one hundred and eight nights.

"Merchant of Venice".	250	performances
"Othello"		
"Romeo and Juliet"	161	,,
"Much Ado about Nothing"	212	,,
"Twelfth Night".		
"Macbeth".	151	,,
"Henry VIII."	203	,,
"King Lear"	72	,,
"Cymbeline"		
"Coriolanus"		

This list is confined to the production of the Shakespearean drama, but there is another list which includes the modern drama, represented by such plays as "The

Bells," "Louis XI.," "Waterloo," "Ravenswood," "The Cup," "Becket," "Lyons Mail," "The Dead Heart," "Robespeare," "Faust," "Madame Sans Gene," "Vicar of Wakefield," "Peter the Great," "Amber Heart," " Richelieu," " King Arthur," and others of less note.

The foregoing catalogue of productions at the Lyceum will give a fair idea of the immense amount of thought and artistic labour involved, and it is satisfactory to know that although the cost involved was great, the return was highly satisfactory and honourable to the taste and appreciation of the playgoers of the latter half of the Victorian Era. A few details of the cost and monetary return of the Lyceum productions are interesting.

In the issue of the *Daily Chronicle*, of September 19th, 1896, we find that Sir Henry told his interviewer that "in the days of Mr. Bateman's management we produced 'Hamlet,' which had the unprecedented run of two hundred nights, *at a net profit of* £10,000. The whole production cost about £100." He also tells us that the "Merchant of Venice" cost only £1,200. "A very small outlay on a picture of Venice."

It is interesting to note what a wide range of scenery, costume, and properties is covered by the foregoing list of Lyceum productions. I am inclined to think that the plays involving Italian, or rather the Venetian, adjuncts and surroundings, and which could be ascertained without surmise or imagination, appealed most strongly to Irving's love of the picturesque. "The Merchant of Venice" gave an opportunity of artistic display which will never be exceeded by any future attempt on the stage. "Henry VIII." was a wonderful production of the pictorial surroundings both in scenery and costume, which, fully rendered, expressed the Holbein idea under its fullest expression. It was in these two plays that the wonderful coalition I have before spoken of, between the two principal actors, produced a result which thoroughly satisfied every lover of the Shakespearean drama; and we all feel thankful to Irving and Ellen Terry for these supreme realisations of the poet's idea. The Shylock of Sir Henry Irving was a revelation, and may be considered a monumental piece of work in the fabric of Victorian Stage art.

The mind of the great actor-manager was fully charged with a love of the Mediæval and Renaissance periods of the history of the Western World, and it was owing to a curious incident that he turned his thoughts to the production of the classic dramas of Shakespeare. The incident was accidental, and I may be pardoned for relating it. During the run of "Hamlet," in 1879, I happened to go into Irving's dressing room after the great scene between Hamlet and his mother. After this arduous piece of work it was the actor's custom to strip and subject the body to a rubbing process. On my entering the dressing room, I found this had been accomplished, and the actor was covered with a white sheet which flowed gracefully to the floor. Irving was standing at his dressing table, and as I entered he flung this white garment around him and said, "What does this remind you of?" Instantly I exclaimed, "Cato!"

my mind realizing a reproduction of the celebrated engraving. Irving said, " Will it do for Coriolanus ? " I replied, " The very thing, ready made up." Before the evening was over we decided to consult Alma Tadema. The next morning we found ourselves in the great painter's house in Regent's Park. He eagerly embraced the idea of making the drawings for Irving's first effort at the production of a classic play of Shakespeare's. The preliminary work was accomplished, and the great painter of classic subjects handsomely rewarded. Alas! for reasons which I must not state, the great classic idea was abandoned ; the fine drawings by Sir Alma Tadema were locked up in the manager's bureau, and we had all to grow older before the play was produced in the year 1901. "Cymbeline" was produced on semi-classic lines; as also " King Lear," under the artistic control of the late Madox Brown, but "Coriolanus" may be considered as the only effort on strictly classic lines of Shakespearean Stage productions at the Lyceum under the management of Sir Henry Irving.

It would be intensely interesting to dwell on the beauties and the histrionic art as developed in the plays outside the Shakespearean productions, but this must be left to the future biographer of Sir Henry Irving. " Richelieu" and " Louis XI." were great and memorable efforts, but my " Notes and Recollections" are mainly associated with the productions of the Tennysonian drama and the " Waterloo" of Dr. Conan Doyle. Irving told me many interesting anecdotes relating to his intercourse and friendship with the great Poet-Laureate of Queen Victoria's reign. It was a matter of no little difficulty to make the poet understand that his beautiful thoughts should be put into such a form as would suit the demands of stage requirements. After considerable discussion Tennyson gave up the fight, and left the matter in the hands of the man who was to undertake the anxiety and risk of production. All lovers of Stage art of our time are thankful for this result, which produced the beautiful play of " The Cup," and the fine play of " Becket," in which the great actor-manager took his leave of the world at Bradford Town, on October 13th, 1905.

Both of these Tennysonian plays have been the medium of accentuating what I have chosen to call the art of the Victorian era, in proof of this I may be pardoned for introducing an account of an incident which occurred on the first night of " The Cup." On this occasion I sat next to Sir Alma Tadema.

The fine temple interior opened an act : the scene was gloomy and sombre ; after a time the temple portal opened, and a ray of daylight burst upon the scene. Then followed a procession of children classically attired, and garlanded with roses ; they danced and sang and ultimately got into position. The *ensemble* was a picture of exquisite classical beauty.

Some of those present were spellbound by the classic realism of this picture. While thunders of applause resounded through the theatre, the first man of the silent ones who spoke was Alma Tadema. With a sigh and a shrug of the shoulders, he exclaimed, "Ah! how poor my art is after this." The great artist repeated this opinion to the great actor-manager. Irving, with that sad smile which sometimes passed across his features, said, "Ah! Tadema, when I am dead and gone my art is gone, while your's lives for ever." This saying impressed us all deeply. The art of the actor can only live in the memory of those who hear and see him, but the art of the great painter will live as long as the creations of Homer, Dante, and Shakespeare.

Another instance of what I have called the accentuation of the art of the Victorian Stage may be recorded.

It will still be fresh in the memory of some of my readers how Sir Henry Irving, by a masterstroke of art, placed the copestone of interest on Herman Merivale's dramatic version of Sir Walter Scott's novel, under the title of "Ravenswood." The author's last lines were spoken ; the curtain closed on the last scene, but only to be quickly raised again on a sunset "cloth," with sea and sandy foreground. Faithful old Caleb Balderstone was discovered picking up the hat and plume : all that remained of his unfortunate master. This scene accentuated the misery and fatality of the drama, and was, therefore, not only a beautiful, but a legitimate adjunct to the play.

I have always held the opinion that when a realistic scene or episode will assist in the accentuation of the author's idea, it is not only admissible but desirable. I recollect a wonderful effect was produced in the trial

scene in the "Winter's Tale," at Manchester. When
Leontes says :

> "There is no truth at all i' the oracle,
> The sessions shall proceed; this is mere falsehood,"

on the utterance of the word "falsehood" a flash of
forked lightning shot across the stage, followed by a
clap of thunder, which brought the audience to their
feet. Shakespeare intended that the blaspheming
mortal should be alarmed and punished by the gods;
hence the following expression :—

> "Apollo's angry ; and the heavens themselves
> Do strike at my injustice."

I daresay some of my readers will smile when I say
that that peal of thunder cost weeks of thought and
mechanical labour ; it was no mere "stage thunder," but
it was as near nature as thought and money could make
it. The result was perfectly legitimate ; the audience
was profoundly impressed, and the poet's leading idea
realised.

There was a phase in Irving's histrionic art which
was of such value and interest that it requires attention
at the hands of any writer who attempts to chronicle the
art work of the great actor. I allude to creative genius,
or the natural power which enables an artist of the
Stage to impersonate an author's meaning for the first
time before an audience.

It should be borne in mind that the actor who
follows his predecessors in a part is more or less
hampered by tradition, and original thought is clouded

by a knowledge of what has been done before. In the case of the creation of a new and original part the actor has a chance of development which does not attend the copyist or follower of a previous artist.

Amid the triumphs of Irving's art life, nothing will transcend the creation of the characters of "Charles the First" or Gregory Brewster in "Waterloo." To the contemporaries of their great delineator they will not only be thought of as works of high art, but they will remain as exquisite memories "as long as memory shall hold her seat." It is a curious thing that the great and true artist does not seem to realize the beauty and importance of his creation. I remember when in December, 1905, Irving turned to me whilst dressing for Brewster, and in consequence of something I had said in a speech at a social gathering in his honour, said, " My friend, you think too highly of ' Waterloo ' ; there cannot be in it what you say." I replied, " You remind me of Joe Jefferson when I spoke to him of that immortal scene on the Catskill mountains, where no one speaks but Rip Van Winkle, and where he kept his back to the audience for at least twenty minutes, and the curtain dropped on rounds of applause. ' Is that so ? ' replied the great actor, ' I did not know I did that.' " Rip Van Winkle and Gregory Brewster will live as long as theatrical annals last.

There are other original parts in the great repertoire of pieces given at the Lyceum including the Tennysonian creations, but that of " Becket " was the most important, and has become sadly memorable ; the great creator of the character may be said to have bid fare-well to the world when he fell at the altar in the last scene of all in the life of the great ecclesiastic.

Sir Henry Irving's work in the art of the Stage is unique in its history, inasmuch as it comprehends a new order of impersonation and has closed the history of the conventional and academic school which lived and lingered some few years in the early part of the Victorian Era. The great results of the Lyceum work are due to two causes. First, the power of conception and the high intellect which enabled the manager to dominate the whole work; and, secondly, to his personality, which carried him into the highest ranks of society and made him beloved in the worlds of literature and art.

It does not come within the scope of this work to chronicle or describe the social methods adopted by Sir Henry Irving to bring together men and women of culture. I trust those who remember those methods have pleasant memories of the stage gatherings on "first nights," when the representatives of culture in art, literature, and society met at the festive board of the genial host. Some of these occasions were memorable in connection with the art of the Victorian Stage; that after the production of "The Merchant of Venice" especially, but this event I have already recorded in my book of "Experiences." At these gatherings came the men who aided the great manager in various ways, and it was a source of pleasure to meet Sir Alma Tadema, R.A., Seymour Lucas, R.A., Madox Brown, and others.

Those who were permanently attached to the Lyceum work always formed part of the gathering, and were represented by Mr. Bram Stoker, H. J. Loveday, Hawes Craven, and others.

On all public occasions when Sir Henry Irving was a guest of a civic or other host, he used the situation to uphold the honour of the Stage as a high medium of artistic expression, and to advance arguments in favour of the establishment of theatres under municipal auspices and control. It may truly be said that by word and action Irving never failed to uphold and advance the art of the Victorian Stage.

It has always seemed to me that one of the most important features of Victorian civilisation is the closer drawing together of the English and American people. Any ill-feeling left by the separation of the two countries has died away and, as a matter of course, the feeling of brotherhood has strengthened ; the two English-speaking people now form the greatest link in the chain of humanity. It is not my intention in this work to indulge in a review of history which has produced such a grand result, but I cannot refrain from a statement that one of the causes of this result is owing to the interchange of social life and cultured refinement. In this respect the art of the Stage has achieved wonders. I consider that the visit of Henry Irving to America, in 1883, was a wonderful means of increasing and consolidating the brotherly feeling between the people of America and England. Irving's progress through the country was a triumphal pro-

cession, whether on or off the Stage, and the affection
of Englishmen for their American brethren is now
registered along with the name of the greatest actor of
the Victorian Era.

When I accompanied my old friend on board the
Britannic on the 11th of October, 1883, I felt some
doubt as to the success of the professional part of the
venture, but that there would be a social success I was
certain.   Those who remember that great Banquet at
the St. James's Hall, London, held out of compliment
to the American people, on the *Fourth of July*, and as
a public farewell to Henry Irving, will not have
forgotten the speech of Lord Coleridge in proposing
the health of the guest of the evening, or that of the
American Ambassador, the Hon. Russell Lowell.
Professor Tyndall and Alma Tadema, R.A., also spoke,
and Sims Reeves, Santley, and Antoinette Stirling
sang in honour of their distinguished friend.   This
event was an admission on the part of those distinguished in art, literature, and science, that the man
they were sending away to America represented the
highest phase of the art of the Victorian Stage.

The professional and social successes of Henry
Irving in America have been well recorded by Mr.
Joseph Hatton in his bright and pleasant two volumes
entitled " Henry Irving's Impressions of America."   I
do not propose, therefore, to enter into detail, but simply
to record that I know Irving's American experiences
were a delight to him and to Ellen Terry also.   In
Mr. Hatton's book, in the preface, there is an address

"To the American Public" by Irving, in which he writes: "In the history of the Stage the Lyceum Company is the first complete organisation which has crossed the Atlantic with the entire equipment of a theatre," and further—to show his appreciation of America, he writes: "I can but trust that I have not erred in expressing for publication some passing thoughts about a country which has excited my profound admiration, and which has the highest claims upon my gratitude."

The visits of Irving and his Lyceum Company to the American Continent ended in artistic and financial results unprecedented in the history of the Theatre. A few facts in connection with the American ventures given to me by Sir Henry may be of interest. At San Francisco they took in fourteen performances £15,000. At Chicago, for two performances in one day of "Louis XI." and the "Merchant of Venice," the receipts amounted to £2,300. This was during the Exhibition time, when the audiences consisted of non-residents. The "Merchant of Venice" *ran for four weeks without a break* in New York, and I do not violate any confidences when I record the fact that Sir Henry Irving cleared by one American venture over £30,000. Shakespeare on this occasion did not spell ruin, and the method of production adopted by Irving was a triumph for the art of the Victorian Stage.

In Irving's farewell speech in America we find the following, as recorded by a biographer: "You have shown that upon the broad platform of a noble art the two greatest sections of the English-speaking race are one nation."

The effect of Irving's work on the stage art of the Victorian Era has been really wonderful. The stage life of the great actor-manager resulted in monumental effort; and the social life of the man produced not only affectionate regard for himself, but a respectful regard for the Theatre as a great and valuable national institution. The change in public appreciation of the Stage as a medium of art expression during the latter half of Queen Victoria's reign forms a phenomenal epoch in the history of the Stage, and is mainly owing to the gigantic work of Sir Henry Irving. This is confirmed by the fact that his life and work were recognised by the honour of knighthood, by the reading of a play in the chapter house of Canterbury Cathedral, and by the conferring of honours of three universities. These honours are conclusive proofs that the art of the Victorian Stage is now fully recognised and appreciated, and that the prejudice against the Theatre in bygone times has been entirely removed. Truly the members of their histrionic profession may feel proud and thankful that the work of the Stage has reached such a high point in public appreciation. The name of the man who wrought this great revolution will be treasured in the future annals of the English Stage.

I have before remarked that I am not writing a biography of Sir Henry Irving, but some events cannot be easily passed over, and I would briefly allude to a farewell banquet given to Sir Henry by the members of the Brasenose Club, Manchester, on the 4th of December, 1904. I was requested to give the health of the guest. This was a pleasant and a difficult task, inasmuch as affectionate regard had to give way to a formal reference to the great work achieved by Sir Henry Irving. I recollect closing my remarks with a quotation from the Immortal Bard.

> "God bless you !
> And send you many years
> Of sunshine days."

Alas! little did we think those days would be so few in number, and that the delightful voice which thanked the assembly would be so soon hushed for ever.

When Henry Irving died, a great man left the world. There could be no doubt of this fact in the mind of anyone on that memorable morning of the twentieth of October, 1905, who was present in or near the grand old Abbey of Westminster. It was an impressive sight, that immense concourse of humanity present at the obsequies of an actor, who found his last resting place in "Poet's Corner." It was a sight to gladden the hearts of all who loved Irving, and who treasure his memory, as one who elevated his art so as to win the admiration and respect of a nation.

The funeral ceremony was grand, solemn, and affecting. I think the supreme moment was reached, when the organ and the brass instruments accompanied the choir in rendering the setting of "Crossing the Bar," by our old friend, Sir Frederick Bridge. This was so exquisite in tone and expression, that many in that great congregation were visbly affected. I was taken by Mr. T. Welch (the well-known comedian) into the chapel of St. Faith; here I was left alone with the ashes of my dear friend and the great actor, to be roused from a fit of abstraction by Bram Stoker. The coffin, covered by a work of art (a pall of laurel leaves), was taken along the cloisters, through the Abbey, and finally lodged in the south transept. It was lowered into its resting place, and, amid solemn silence, the Dean pronounced the benediction with exquisite feeling and solemnity. With a last look we left the remains of Henry Irving at the feet of Shakespeare and alongside David Garrick.

Winding my way through the cloisters I fell into a train of thought as to the future of the histrionic art in England, and it occurred to me that the coming generation of actors might take courage from those lines in Longfellow's beautiful " Psalm of Life."

> " Lives of great men all remind us
> We can make our lives sublime,
> And, departing, leave behind us
> Footprints on the Sands of time."

William Winter, a much valued and respected American critic, has written in the *New York Tribune* what I consider amounts to a beautiful and reverential epitaph on Sir Henry Irving.

" Henry Irving lived to bless mankind, and in his death—which is a universal bereavement—he leaves an immortal memory of genius and goodness, and an immortal example of all that is heroic and beautiful in the conduct of life."*

I close my notes and recollections of Henry Irving by quoting some beautiful lines which appeared in the American *Century Magazine.*

EXIT—SIR HENRY IRVING.

Life's act is o'er; Westminster rings;
No more he'll play the numbered kings
    Deposed by Death, exacting
For there where Albion's kings are made,
Now buried with the kings he played,
    Is Henry, King of acting.

He played them well, each in his part;
The Abbey's dead lives in his art,
    Restored unto the throne;
And now his myriad self he brings
Where all the silent, coffined kings
    Receive him as their own.

Time gave his cue, he dropped the role,
And cast the semblance from his soul;
    He is himself at last;
And 'neath the Abbey's sculptured stage
He's conned of life the final page
    With players of the past.

—Charles D. Stewart, in the "January Century."

* From Mr. Austin Brereton's book, entitled "Henry Irving," 1905.

CHAPTER VII.

SIR HENRY IRVING'S CONTEMPORARIES IN SHAKESPEAREAN
PRODUCTION.

ALTHOUGH Mr. Herbert Beerbohm Tree is still
producing in this Edwardian Era Shakespearean
and modern drama work of a high order of merit, I
must include him in the list of those who have helped
in the making of the Stage art of the Victorian epoch.
Her Majesty's Theatre, in the Haymarket, has become
historic as a medium of expression of high dramatic
art ; and I trust may so continue as His Majesty's, and
prolong the good work through the reign of Edward
VII.

My first meeting with Mr. Beerbohm Tree was on
an interesting social occasion in 1878. Geflowski, the
Polish sculptor, had become so successful, that he found
it necessary and desirable to remove into the studio
No. 13, Bruton Street, Berkeley Square, and just
vacated by Noble. The event of removal was celebrated by a sort of art conversazione. The walls were
hung with important examples of the work of contemporary painters. The card of invitation was
designed by Caton Woodville, probably now the most

masterly draughtsman of our time.   Musicians of note
added their delightful art to the entertainment, and
Beerbohm Tree made one of his early bows as a reciter.
How little one can divine the future of individuals : at
that festive gathering little did I think I should in after
years become acquainted with " The Ballad Monger,"
" Captain Swift," " Hamlet," " The Parish Priest," and
other masterpieces of acting by the genial reciter of
that evening.   The gathering of guests was a large
one, and embraced men of note in the aristocratic and
artistic worlds.

In dealing with Tree's contribution to the art of
the Victorian Stage it is necessary to treat of it in two
portions.   The first part is that which embraces the
production of original modern drama at the Haymarket
from 1887 to the period when Her Majesty's Theatre
came into Tree's possession in 1896.   The second
portion commences with the first production in April
of 1897, and must necessarily include the work done up
to the present time.

My notes and recollections on the earlier part of
Tree's career are scanty, and my personal intercourse
with the actor-manager of Her Majesty's Theatre has
been principally confined to the visits of the company
to the City of Manchester.   Although I was present at
Mr. Tree's first production of " Hamlet " in 1891, and
was much impressed by the original treatment of the
character of Hamlet, it seems to me that I have derived
supreme delight in watching those parts and characters

which are the result of the actor's creative genius.   In saying this I do not for one moment wish to convey the idea that the great Shakespearean parts have failed in their impersonation, but, like other great actors, Tree has had the opportunity of creating parts in the modern drama which have no anterior representatives.   The production of the dramatised version of Du Maurier's "Trilby" was an event never to be forgotten by those who saw it.   In this work the part of Svengali fully illustrated that high creative power of the actor to which I have alluded, and also of the actress who portrayed the difficult and unusual part of Trilby.   Miss Dorothea Baird is a name which will always remain on the roll of dramatic annals as that of a young woman of creative genius.   "The Ballad Monger" was another creative effort of Tree's, backed up by the beautiful portrayal of the heroine by Miss Julia Neilson.   Other original efforts in histrionic art consolidated the career of Herbert Beerbohm Tree, and led the way to that responsible and arduous undertaking of the second portion of work I have alluded to, and which has comprised the management and responsibility of Her Majesty's Theatre.

In treating of this part of the work of the actor, and its influence on the art of the Victorian Era, it may be well to give a list of the Shakespearean Revivals and of the original work of the modern dramatist.

The Shakespearean Work, at Her Majesty's, commenced with :

"Julius Cæsar"   .   .   .   .   Jan. 22, 1898.
    followed by

"King John" .   .   .   .   .   Sept. 20, 1899.
"A Midsummer Night's Dream"   .   Jan. 10, 1900.
"Twelfth Night"   .   .   .   .   Feb.   5, 1901.
"The Merry Wives of Windsor"   .   June 10, 1902.
"Richard II." .   .   .   .   .   Sept. 10, 1903.
"The Tempest"   .   .   .   .   Sept. 14, 1904.
"Much Ado about Nothing"   .   .   Jan. 24, 1905.

    Original Work of the Modern Drama:

"The Seats of the Mighty"   .   .   April 28, 1897.
"The Silver Key" .   .   .   .   July 10, 1897.
"Rip Van Winkle" .   .   .   .   May   30, 1900.
"Herod". .   .   .   .   .   Oct. 31, 1900.
"The Last of the Dandies"   .   .   Oct. 24, 1901.
"Ulysses"   .   .   .   .   .   Feb.   1, 1902.
"The Eternal City". .   .   .   Oct.   2, 1902.
"Resurrection"   .   .   .   .   Feb. 17, 1903.
"The Darling of the Gods"   .   .   Dec. 28, 1903.
"Business is Business"   .   .   .   May   13, 1905.
"Oliver Twist"   .   .   .   .   July 10, 1905.
"Nero" .   .   .   .   .   .   —   1906.

These lists do not include many interesting histrionic efforts prior to the work at the Haymarket Theatre. I had the satisfaction of seeing Tree in "Henry IV.," in the part of Hotspur, and treasure the lithographic portrait he gave me as a souvenir of the production. Louis Calvert was the Falstaff. One of the pleasing things about Mr. Tree's Shakespearean work is the association with Louis Calvert, the son of the celebrated Shakespearean revivalist—Charles Alexander Calvert. I recollect when " Henry IV." was played in Manchester, the members of the Brazenose Club celebrated this work of collaboration by a banquet given to Tree, Calvert, Lal Brough, and Gilbert Parker (now Sir Gilbert). This was on September 1st, 1896. On this occasion it fell to my lot to propose the toast of " The Guests." The occasion was pleasant and remarkable. The replies of the guests were admirable, and the author of " The Seats of the Mighty " was greeted with much enthusiasm, and good Lionel Brough delighted the company with his funny tales and comic recitations.

The Shakespearean productions of Herbert Beerbohm Tree have played an important part in the art of the Victorian Stage—some of them stand unrivalled in this line of art—and must be regarded as cultured and courageous efforts to display the works of our great dramatist to the best and highest advantage.

The interpretation of " Julius Cæsar " both from a scenic and histrionic point of view was admirable ; in this work the scholar and the painter produced a correct setting, through which Tree and his fellow actors gave the thrilling situations and the immortal text with consummate art. In " The Tempest" the actor-manager, not being tied down by archæological or architectural demands, plunged into a poetic and pictorial representation of a drama played out on an " enchanted isle." The effect of the opening scene was a triumph of stage management and resource. It is curious that two actor-managers of the Victorian Era should have selected " The Tempest" as a medium of the pictorial expression of Stage art, and that the result should have been the complete realisation of the exquisite beauty of the drama. Charles Alexander Calvert and Herbert Beerbohm Tree have earned the heartfelt thanks of Shakespearean playgoers of the latter half of the Victorian Era.

The production of " The Merry Wives of Windsor," at His Majesty's Theatre, may be regarded as the greatest triumph of Stage art for which Tree is responsible; indeed, in some respects it was an unique effort and will dwell in the memory as a bright spot in the great picture of the Shakespearean revivals of our time, and I class it with the art of the Victorian Stage. Not often in the history of the actor's art is seen such a combination as that including Ellen Terry and Mrs. Kendall as the Merry Wives, with Tree as Falstaff. Nothing that I remember in the Stage art of Victoria's reign has equalled or surpassed this wonderful coalition of histrionic genius; and I am thankful that this fact has been so finely perpetuated, for future generations to look at, in the canvas of the Hon. John Collier. The modern Stage is proud of Ellen Terry and Madge Robertson, and in acting together in Tree's production of the " Merry Wives " a result was produced unique in the history of the art of the English Stage.

In the production of the original modern drama which may be associated with the Victorian period of

Stage art, Tree has done great and good service to his profession. The dramatic work of Sir Gilbert Parker, Stephen Phillips, and Hall Caine has been given with full and truthful stage setting; a dramatised version entitled " Oliver Twist " has worthily echoed the genius of the great novelist in the ears of thousands of play-goers of this Edwardian Era of dramatic art. Herbert Beerbohm Tree has been a worthy contemporary of Sir Henry Irving in the great work of elevating and ennobling the art of the Stage ; he deserves and has the highest regards and the grateful thanks of those who believe in the Stage as a medium of expression for the highest art of the drama.

Frank R. Benson is another contemporary of Irving, who has devoted the prime years of his life to producing and maintaining the best art of the stage. Although not a " Revivalist " as the term has been used hitherto, Benson has produced Shakespeare and the modern drama in a way which has won the appreciation and approval of all lovers of histrionic art.

Placed as I have been in connection with the art of the Theatre, it will not be a matter of surprise that I have had some pleasant experiences with many persons who have adorned, and whose lives are still honourable to, the English Stage. I have even been so vain and idiotic as to imagine I could take my share in the management of a theatre. The result made me a sadder and a wiser man. The only consolation remaining from the disaster is the fact that it brought me the acquaintance of my friend, F. R. Benson. When the theatrical ship was sinking, he appeared for the first time in Manchester, with his company, in a round of Shakespearean pieces. Commencing with "Hamlet," he made a bid for the high position he now occupies in English Stage art, and saved the "Comedy" undertaking from bankruptcy.

What a mass of work Benson has accumulated since those youthful far-off days at the Manchester Theatre! Organizing what has been called the "Benson Repertoire Company," an attempt was made to gather together young men and women of culture who had a desire for the Stage and the art of the Theatre. Benson being a gentleman of high culture and refinement has gathered around his theatrical standard, from year to year, a company of actors who have been able to deal with the portrayal of Shakespearean characters; and also with those of high-class modern drama and old English comedy.

In order that a fair idea may be formed of the work done for the Victorian Stage by Benson I will include the following list :—

Shakespearean Productions.

"Hamlet"	"Romeo and Juliet"
"Macbeth"	"Othello"
"Merchant of Venice"	"As You Like It"
"Much Ado about Nothing"	"Taming of the Shrew"
"Twelfth Night"	"Comedy of Errors"
"King Lear"	"Julius Cæsar"
"Antony and Cleopatra"	"Pericles"

"Timon of Athens"   "Coriolanus"
"Winter's Tale"   "Merry Wives of Windsor"
"The Tempest"   "King John"
"Richard II."   "Henry VI." (Part 1)
"Henry IV." (Part 1)   "Henry VI." (Part 2)
"Henry IV." (Part 2)   "Henry VI." (Part 3)
"Henry V."   "Richard III."
"Midsummer Night's   "Henry VIII."
    Dream"

This is an honourable record of the work of an actor-manager in placing twenty-nine of the immortal plays of Shakespeare on the English Stage, and presenting them in all parts of the country.

The following list will show what Benson has done for the modern drama, much of it representative work of the last half of the Victorian epoch:

> "The Orestean Trilogy of Aeschylus"
> "Edward II." (Marlowe)
> "Every Man in his Humour"
> "Diarmid and Grania" (Moore and Yeates)
> "Money"
> "School for Scandal"
> "She Stoops to Conquer"
> "The Rivals"
> "Aylmer's Secret" (Stephen Phillips)
> "Paola and Frencesca" (Stephen Phillips)
> "Lady of Lyons" (Lytton)
> "Richelieu" (Lytton)
> "Garrick"

" A Foregone Conclusion"

" King Rene's Daughter"

" The Belle's Strategem"

" Corsican Brothers"

" Our Bitterest Foe"

" Still Waters Run Deep"

" New Men and Old Acres"

" Robert Macaire"

" Heart of Midlothian"

" Rob Roy"

" Sheep in Wolf's Clothing"

In addition to the labour and expense involved in the production and playing of the foregoing dramatic works, Benson has been responsible, for the last dozen years, for the carrying out and the success of the Shakespeare Festivals at Stratford-on-Avon, in honour of the poet's birthday; and on a repetition of these Festivals this year Benson will produce the three parts of "Henry VI." complete.

An interesting feature of Benson's work is its educational character. He has endeavoured to create a love of the classic drama outside the walls of the Theatre, and an audience has been created to support and appreciate high-class work, when given on the boards of a theatre or as a theatrical venture. The "Trilogy" in the foregoing list has been taken on a special tour round to most of the public schools of England, and afterwards given before a London audience.

In estimating the value of the work of Frank R Benson in the art of the Victorian Stage, it should be borne in mind that he has not sought to become what is called a "revivalist" of Shakespeare, but strictly a "producer" on cultured and educational lines. From such a standpoint of appreciation Benson stands unrivalled in the history of dramatic art, and deserves the heartfelt thanks of a nation which produced the immortal genius which it is the object of his life to interpret and illustrate through the medium of the English Stage.

In writing of the scheme which was discussed some years ago for the creation and endowment of a national theatre, in a New York evening paper in the year 1901, the writer has justly summed up the value and importance of Benson's theatrical work. He says :—

Perhaps the day for the laying of the foundation stone may not be so far distant as it now seems to be. There are some faint signs, delusive perhaps, but promising, of the revival of the drama in England, and any quickening of the spirit there, would soon be reflected here. While other folk have been talking of the need of a national theatre, Mr. Frank R. Benson has been doing his best to supply one, and has been successful at least in showing, by practical demonstration, the proper genesis of such an organisation. This young enthusiast, still in the prime of manhood, is at the head of the best English speaking stock company in the world, laboriously wrought out of raw material, and he has done more to popularise Shakespeare in the British Isles, than any man of his day and generation, Sir Henry Irving not excepted. In the way of Shakespearean production, indeed, he has probably beaten all records of the past century, save only those of that great actor-manager, Samuel Phelps, and even he never dared to give, as Mr. Benson has given, a performance of Hamlet, with the full text.

.   .   .   .   .   .

In any case, Mr. Benson has proved that the higher drama can be played, profitably, year in year out, without stars, without spectacle, and without much advertisement, but solely upon its merits. Mr. Phelps proved the same thing fifty years ago in the uncultivated district of Islington. The public taste now, as then, is sound in this matter. But no one wants to see great plays badly acted. The resuscitation of the higher drama is hopeless without performers superior in training and capacity to those who now occupy the stage. There is some ground for the hope that they may be forthcoming. The number of young college students adopting the stage as a serious profession has become considerable, and is increasing. Possibly they may supply the new blood, and the genuinely artistic ambitions, that are needed to make the scheme of a national theatre practicable. When one is built, Mr. Benson would be a good man to put in charge of it."

When we think of the past history and vicissitudes of the drama in this country, we are able to realize what has been achieved by such actor-managers as Charles Kean, Samuel Phelps; Charles Calvert, Henry Irving, Beerbohm Tree, and Frank R. Benson.

We can with difficulty believe that when our immortal dramatist wrote, the names of the scenes of his plays were written on boards and hoisted over the platform, and that every character, whether Greek, Roman, or mediæval, was habited in the costume of the Elizabethan era.

In Shakespeare's time the "players" had no social repute ; they were strollers on the face of the earth ; now they are honoured by all, from the gracious Sovereign on the throne to the hard-working son of toil. How has this wonderful change been brought about? I venture to say that it is owing to the culture and enthusiasm of the men who took up the art of the Stage on Macready's retirement, and who have spent their best energies and the best part of their lives in bringing the genius of Shakespeare home to the English people, by illustration and exposition on the lines I have advocated in these pages. Let us, then, thankfully acknowledge the services rendered to art by the actor-managers of our time; and especially when we remember that they have been rendered in honour of that great genius whose work they have loved and illustrated so beautifully.

CHAPTER VIII.

ROBERTSONIAN AND MODERN DRAMA.

IN considering the art of the Victorian Stage from a histrionic point of view, it is necessary to review the work of the Stage anterior to the advent of the Robertsonian drama. I have hitherto dealt almost exclusively with the art of the "Revivalist" and "Producer" of the Shakespearean and high-class drama. The other phase of dramatic art embraces the representation of plays by appropriate action, and with a " mounting " sufficient to express the scenes in which the action takes place. It will therefore be admitted that this phase of dramatic art must depend for success on the author and the men and women of histrionic genius who give Stage expression to his work.

There have been many fine actors and actresses in the period between the Kembles and the Robertsonian drama. It is a difficult matter to chronicle and explain the work of this period to the present generation of twentieth century playgoers. The names of Gustavus Vaughan Brooke, Charles Dillon, Barry Sullivan, Charles Mathews, Madame Vestris, Coleman, and

Swinbourne may be taken as representing the good
work of the anti-Robertson period ; the greatest artiste
was Helen Faucit (Lady Martin).   Her name may be
placed alongside that of Sarah Siddons as the exponent
of the beautiful, the grand, and the noble art of the first
part of the reign of Queen Victoria.   The life and work
of Helen Faucit have been written of by her husband,
Sir Theodore Martin, therefore, with such a book in
existence, it is not necessary to go into the detail of the
work of this gifted actress ; there are, however, within
my own recollection certain histrionic results to which I
may allude.

My first sight of Helen Faucit was on the stage of
the Theatre Royal, Manchester, in 1866, on which
occasion she was supported by dear old Howe of the
old Haymarket company.   The play was "Cymbeline."
It seems to me desirable that the triumphs of the actor
should be placed on record, in order that future
generations may know how hearts have been moved by
the representation of human passions through the
medium of histrionic genius.   In the portrayal of
Imogen there were soul-stirring moments so intense and
which became so impressed on the mind that the lapse of
time cannot even dim, much less efface them from the
tablets of the brain.   I recall that memorable scene between Imogen and Iachimo.   After the villain had tried
the patience of the good woman and faithful wife to the
uttermost she turned her back on the man, but on the
exclamation " Let me my service tender on your lips,"
that magnificent figure wheeled round and, in a voice

of thundering scorn, cried out "Away! I do condemn mine ears that have so long attended thee." I shall never forget that "Away!" It brought Iachimo to his knees and the audience to its feet. It evoked a shout of applause which I venture to think has never been exceeded within the walls of a theatre. It was a deafening tribute of appreciation for a great and good woman as embodied by the actress.

Although Helen Faucit was supreme in tragedy she was fascinating and victorious in comedy. I have already alluded to her Rosalind in "As You Like It," which gave us everything that Shakespeare intended, and which revealed the beauty and fascinating influence of the queen of comedy.

In rendering the part of Iolanthe in "King Rene's Daughter" (a play written by Sir Theodore Martin from a Danish version of the piece) Helen Faucit reached the summit of poetic beauty in histrionic art. The refinement and grace of the blind girl's movements and her tender and musical voice produced a result which will ever dwell in the memory.

Helen Faucit acted for the last time as Rosalind at the Calvert Memorial Performances in 1879 before alluded to, and was laid to rest in the Brompton Cemetery in 1898. A distinguished throng paid a reverential respect to the noble woman, and to the greatest actress of the Victorian Stage.

It is a curious and interesting fact that at one theatre in the metropolis the spirit of the true art of comedy was kept alive. There are still living persons who remember the Haymarket company under the control and management of John Baldwin Buckstone. Associated with this company were Howe, Chippendale, Compton, Fanny Rodgers, Louisa Angell, and others. This company, in the late fifties and early sixties, kept alive the spirit of true comedy in spite of the growing influence of farce and extravaganza. A recollection of the old English comedies, such as " The Rivals," " She Stoops to Conquer," and " The School for Scandal," represented by the Haymarket Company is pleasant, and reminds many old playgoers of what they choose to call the grand old days of half a century ago.

There can be no doubt as to the cause of the decline of taste for pure comedy, This was the advent of Edward Askew Sothern as a member of the Haymarket Company, and to the production of a piece which gave him the opportunity of creating a part which has rendered his name famous and immortal amongst the English-speaking playgoers of the world. The late Tom Taylor (with whom I had a delightful acquaintance, and who helped me to produce the Calvert Memorial Performances in 1879) wrote a piece which he entitled "Our American Cousin," and sent it over to America with a view to its production in New York. It was not considered a brilliant example of dramatic art, but Laura Keen at last determined to produce it, with Joseph Jefferson as Asa Trenchard, and Sothern in the small part of Lord Dundreary. It is interesting to note that two actors, who have risen to the highest point of honour in the modern art of the Stage, should thus meet in the cast of a drama written by an English author. As long as dramatic annals survive, Rip Van Winkle and Lord Dundreary will appear in letters of gold, enclosed with the victorious wreaths offered by the brotherhood of England and America.

As Lord Dundreary was a creation absolutely unique in the history of the art of the Stage, it is desirable to offer explanatory words on its origin and history.

Writing of the production of "Our American Cousin," Joseph Jefferson, in his autobiography, says :—

"The Abel Murcott of Mr. Couldock was a gem, and the extravagant force and humour of Mr. Sothern's Dundreary, the fame of which afterwards resounded all over the English-speaking world, is too well known to need any comment, except, perhaps, to mention one or two matters connected with it of a curious nature.

As I have before said, Sothern was much dejected at being compelled to play the part. He said he could do nothing with it, and certainly for the first two weeks it was a dull effort and produced but little effect. So in despair he began to introduce extravagant business into his character, skipping about the stage, stammering and sneezing, and, in short, doing all he could to attract and distract the attention of the audience. To the surprise of everyone, himself included, these antics, intended by him to injure the character, were received by the audience with delight. He was a shrewd man as well as an effective actor, and he saw at a glance that accident had revealed to him a golden opportunity. He took advantage of it, and with cautious steps increased his speed, feeling the ground well under him as he proceeded. Before the first month was over he stood side by side with any other character in the play; and at the end of the run he was, in my opinion, considerably in advance of us all.

And his success in London in the same character fully attests, whatever may be said to the contrary, that as an extravagant eccentric comedian in the modern range of comedy he was quite without a rival.

His performance of Sam which I saw at the Haymarket Theatre, in London, was a still finer piece of acting than his Dundreary. It was equally strong, and had the advantage of the other in not being overdrawn or extravagant."

If I remember rightly, the repertoire of the old Haymarket Company began to show signs of decline in public favour, and, in 1861, "Our American Cousin" was accepted by Buckstone, and produced with himself in the part of Asa Trenchard. It was in the great exhibition year of 1862 that I first saw Sothern's Lord Dundreary ; at that time it had become the wonder of the Stage, and all the English-speaking world crowded the Haymarket nightly to see the wonderful creation of histrionic art.

The creation and completion of the character of *Lord Dundreary* is the most curious incident in histrionic art hitherto witnessed on the English Stage. Unlike other stage creations, which are the result of a carefully thought out scheme of delineation, *Lord Dundreary* was built up, developed and perfected on accident. When the part was originally placed in Sothern's hands by Laura Keen in America, he was disappointed and thought little of the part. With a view to get rid of it, he introduced a burlesque treatment, including the idiotic skipping about the stage, the stammer and the sneeze. Instead of damning the character, this treatment of the weak, English aristocrat caused laughter and pleasure,

and our American brethren passed on the impersonation a verdict of approval by acclamation. The brother
Sam allusions, although ludicrously absurd in themselves,
provoked laughter, and the reading of Sam's letter was
a complete work of art ; and when Dundreary read the
lines relative to brother Sam having purchased an
estate, in which he wrote, " The enclosed pill box con-
tains a sample of the soil," the audience burst into a fit
of laughter and applause. The scenes with *Georgina*
were absurdly comic; but one of the most original
features of the part, was the happy idea of introducing
proverbial expressions and then stopping to analyse
them ; those who remember the analysis of the proverb,
" Birds of a feather flock together," will understand that
I am quite justified in saying that the character of
Dundreary, as created and completed by Edward Askew
Sothern, has become immortal in the Stage annals of
this country.

In stage production change is necessary sooner or
later, even during the run of a successful piece ; and so,
after a triumphant run on the time-honoured boards of
the Haymarket Theatre, " Our American Cousin " was
removed for other pieces, which, in addition to
" Brother Sam," were intended to afford Sothern a
chance of showing that his histrionic powers were not
confined to the portrayal of the half-idiotic aristocrat.
This change was the means of bringing about a class of
dramatic writing before totally unknown to the Stage.
With the advent of T. W. Robertson as a writer for
the Stage a new state of things theatrical was created,

by which his name as a dramatist has been rendered immortal, and which inaugurated a red-letter epoch in the history of Victorian Stage art.

Robertson's success as a dramatic author commenced with his work for the Prince of Wales' Theatre, in Tottenham Street, but he produced pieces for the Haymarket Theatre after Sothern had played in such pieces as "My Aunt's Advice" and "The Little Treasure" (in which Ellen Terry was the *Gertrude*). It was, however, in "David Garrick" by Robertson that he made his second great success as an actor, and added another feature of interest to the Victorian Stage.

The history of Robertson's play of "David Garrick" is interesting. It was bought by a dramatic publisher for a small sum, and after lying dormant for many years was heard of by Sothern, who determined Garrick should succeed *Dundreary*. In the memoir of Sothern, written by my late friend, T. Edgar Pemberton, I find it stated that the piece was first presented in Birmingham. In London it produced a great impression, and I remember the consummate art with which Sothern endeavoured to disenchant Ada Ingot, the daughter of a London alderman, by feigning inebriation. It was plain to the audience that Garrick was sorry to do this, and it was a sad thing for the young woman to find that the great actor, the object of her adoration, should be guilty of such depravity. The art of the actor in this scene of simulated inebriation rose to the highest point of excellence, and established the success of a piece adapted by a comparatively unknown dramatist. The play has, since Sothern's time, commanded enthusiastic audiences when *Garrick* has been enacted by Charles Wyndham and Edward Compton, but the work of the creator of the part will ever live in the history of the Victorian Stage.

Before closing his association with the Haymarket and Sothern, "Tom Robertson" adapted "Home" and "Birth," but the time was shortly to come when the English world was to see original, and most beautiful work, rendered by a set of consummate artists, who immediately became identified with the new phase of dramatic literature, inaugurated and perfected by Thomas William Robertson.

The taking of the little Queen's Theatre, in Tottenham Street, by Marie Wilton, with H. J. Byron as helpmate, was one of those events which mark great epochs in the history of the drama and the art of the Stage. After getting possession of the theatre, Marie Wilton obtained permission to change the name to "The Prince of Wales," and thus linking, as it were, the royal title of the heir apparent with one of the most extraordinary adventures of the Victorian era. It was a serious and hazardous undertaking; the place was distant and of no repute, but the courage and determination of the lessee effected a transformation, and the theatre was opened after alterations, new decoration and furnishing, carried out in such a manner as to be a revelation to the playgoers of nearly half a century ago.

Marie Wilton had certain business relations with H. J. Byron, and which resulted in the talented lady coming in contact with T. W. Robertson. Byron and he were great friends, and the former, anxious to do the latter a good turn, an original drama of his was submitted for Marie Wilton's approval. "Tom Robertson" had undergone many trials and disappointments, and this same play had been refused by Buckstone at the Haymarket. Much interesting information on the production of this play, called "Society," may be obtained from Edgar Pemberton's "Life and Writings of Robertson," and from the book of the Bancroft's, by Sir Squire and Lady Bancroft, the Marie Wilton of the Prince of Wales Theatre.

The eleventh of November, 1865, was a memorable day in the history of the art of the English Stage. On this day, Robertson's "Society" was produced at the Prince of Wales Theatre, and revealed a troop of actors who might have been specially created to portray the beauties of the Robertsonian characters. Besides Marie Wilton, the names of Hare, Trafford, Bancroft, Ray, John Clarke, Dewar Montgomery, Hill, Tindale Bennett, and Miss Larkin appear in the first cast of "Society." As the Robersonian drama progressed, other names of historic interest were added to the list of its delineators, such as Lydia Foote, Ada Dyas, George Honey, and Younge.

The Robertsonian drama afforded ample opportunity for the creation of original character. The fact was evident in the wonderful revelation of character by John Hare, Bancroft, George Honey and John Clarke. In the case of Hare, it may be truly said, that his fame as an actor was made and consolidated by the characters he developed in the Robertsonian drama.

In the history of the English Stage, the Robertsonian epoch is the most wonderful. A complete change was created in dramatic material, and a new order of actors was cast for its exposition. On that memorable night in November, 1865, when "Society" was produced by that courageous lady of the Prince of Wales Theatre in Tottenham Court Road, a new order of histrionic art was established, which carried English men and women along like a torrent, and brought a financial reward to its struggling author and to those responsible for a plucky theatrical venture. The dramatic work of Robertson was the death blow to that conventionality which lingered as a legacy of the old school; henceforth, all was to be a reflex of human nature, in its joys and sorrows, framed in beautiful "mounting" and expounded by a new order of histrionic genius. A volume might well be written on this period of Victorian Stage art, but I can only deal with it "from notes and recollections."

The Robertsonian drama is represented by the plays entitled, " Society," " Ours," " Caste," " Play," and "School." Although all are admirable, I think "Caste" may be considered the masterpiece; although the acting of all was of the highest order, I am inclined to conclude that the actors and actresses reached the acme of the newly founded school of histrionic art, in the piece which dealt with the loves of Esther and Polly Eccles for the Hon. George D'Alroy and Sam Gerridge, the plumber. The two charming sisters were played by Lydia Foote

and Marie Wilton (now Lady Bancroft). Robertson
had a peculiar way occasionally of relying upon action
only, accompanied by no vocal efforts. Some playgoers
now living will not have forgotten some scenes of this
description. I shall always remember the scene where
George D'Alroy endeavoured to cheer his wife, and
encourage her to bear the pain of his departure for the
war, by asking her to buckle on his sword and belt.
I recollect the last time I saw this scene the wife was
played by my dear old friend Ada Dyas, whose
acquaintance I made at the tercentenary celebration of
Shakespeare's birth, when I played Jaques to her
Rosalind in a Lancashire town. Those who saw Ada
Dyas try to buckle on that sword and belt will never
forget the force of expression conveyed by action and
facial working. The effort was made with a breaking
heart, and with the fearful thought she might never see
her husband again. The effort left her a sad and
grief-laden woman. The audience saw and understood
this and, as Esther fell fainting into the arms of those
who loved her, rose to the situation with prolonged
applause. Another instance of this peculiar trait in the
Robertsonian drama may be cited. On D'Alroy's
return he finds that those near and dear to him have
been cared for in their poverty and distress, and that
various household comforts have been provided. On
asking how this had happened all heads are turned to
the man who believed in caste and who, in a conceited
aristocratic style, had ridiculed his friend's affection for
the daughter of a plebeian drunken reprobate. D'Alroy

walked up to his friend, Captain Hawtrey, and in dead silence grasped him by the hand. If any words *were* spoken they were drowned in applause. From that moment the audience loved the man on whom they had looked as a conceited nincompoop. Such is the power of genius when dealing with the exposition of intensity in human nature. This scene has painted on the mental canvas the portrait of F. Younge and Mr. Bancroft (now Sir Squire Bancroft) that can only be effaced in the land of shadows.

Probably, no drama written in the Victorian era has developed the actors' genius in such an extraordinary manner as "Caste." There are only seven characters in the piece, and yet every one of these was developed into a sparkling gem of true art. The drunken father of the two dear girls, Esther and Polly Eccles, became a work of supreme art in the hands of George Honey, and John Hare reached the highest point in his creative art in the good-hearted plumber, Sam Gerridge. Miss Larkin was the perfect aristocrat as the Marquise de Saint Maur. Marie Wilton (now Lady Bancroft) was supreme in the good-natured, sparkling Polly, and in artistic contrast to the refined, almost sad nature of her sister Esther (Lydia Foote), who had married the Hon. George D'Alroy.

To all lovers of true dramatic art the creation and exposition of the Robertsonian drama is a source of consolation ; and at the time of its production and continuance at the Prince of Wales' Theatre it supplied a want which was not forthcoming from the contemporary work of the stage.

We shall not see another such revolution in the art of the stage; therefore let us hold in honour the memory of Thomas William Robertson, along with that of those gifted men and women who have gone to "that bourne from whence no traveller returns;" and maintain our respect and admiration for those who are still living, and reposing on well-earned laurels and royal appreciation.

In the development of the stage art of the latter portion of the Victorian era, women of genius have played an important and interesting part It is also interesting to note that female parts requiring creative genius in exposition, have been the works of the modern dramatist.

Miss Genevieve Ward as a creative artist stands out in bold relief against the fabric of Victorian Stage Art. Although an American, she has been so closely allied with the art of the English Stage that we claim her as a member of the histrionic school of this country.

The whirligig of Time is a curious piece of mechanism producing strange and unlooked-for results. I was once sitting beside Genevieve Ward on the stage of the Theatre Royal, Manchester, watching a rehearsal of an act of "King Arthur." I reminded the tragedienne that I saw her first appearance on the same boards (after she had abandoned the Lyric stage) as Lady Macbeth. I refrain from recording the date of this event, but I well remember the discussion at the time on the merits of the performance, and whether the new Lady Macbeth would take a high place on the dramatic stage. Miss Ward's career is historic, and needs no comment from me ; but it is a curious coincidence that when I first saw the new Lady Macbeth of our time, in the person of Ellen Terry, I found myself sitting next to Miss Ward in the stalls of the Lyceum.

I have several pleasant recollections of my intercourse with Miss Ward. I remember when my friend, the late Lewis Wingfield, wrote a play, he induced the talented actress to produce it. This was accordingly done at the Queen's Theatre, Manchester, in June of 1875. The title was "Despite the World," a new romantic play, in two parts and four tableaux. I remember we all worked hard at the production of this ill-fated drama ; Miss Ward did everything that could be done with the heroine Thecla, but in spite of its many literary qualities it would not draw and had to be taken off. I remember Miss Ward thought so highly of her part that she christened a little favourite black dog "Thecla ;" of which she tells an amusing story. Certain royal personages visiting her one evening at the theatre, the little animal showed signs of dislike by growling from his snug retreat in a silk-cushioned basket. Its mistress exclaimed, "Down, Teck ! down, instantly!!" There was much laughter at this, and Miss Ward had to explain to one of the royal personages that the animal was called after poor Wingfield's heroine Thecla.

Miss Ward accepted the responsibility of the management of the Lyceum during a temporary absence of Sir Henry Irving in 1879. I recollect a piece was produced which failed to attract, and the situation became serious. Miss Ward told me one morning on the Lyceum stage that she had a drama which had been laid by some time, and that she had serious thoughts of producing it. The piece was "Forget-me-not," by Grove and Herman Merivale. It was produced, and with a startling result. Stephanie, in this drama, was a creation and a phenomenal success. The part has been played over two thousand times, and "everywhere where English is spoken," Miss Ward has told an interviewer. It is curious how theatrical managers may be mistaken as to the quality or chance of success of plays submitted for their consideration. "Forget-me-not" is not the only play that has been consigned to the oblivion of a manager's bureau, and after many years been accidentally unearthed as a *dernier-ressort* to retrieve loss and disaster.

It is no part of my duty in these pages to chronicle the legal quarrel, which ensued out of the production of "Forget-me-not," between the authors and the great actress; suffice it to say that my old friend, the late Herman Merivale, disapproved of the production, and legal disputes took place. The fact, however, remains, that Genevieve Ward played her great part of Stephanie through the English-speaking world, and materially enhanced the artistic value of the English Stage during the Victorian era.

In the character of Stephanie, Marquise de Mohrivart, the actress found that kind of solid dramatic power she loved so much, and which she has sought in

the selection of parts to be found in the modern, and
older high-class drama. Genevieve Ward's name is
associated with that of Charles Alexander Calvert in
the last great Shakespearean revival in Manchester.
"Henry VIII" was produced at the Theatre Royal in
September, 1877, with Miss Ward as Queen Catherine.
Those who saw this personification will always remember
the council chamber scene, where the queen pleads before
the king, the scene with Cardinal Wolsey, and the
vision and death scene, which placed the cope-stone of
the highest art on this great historical drama. It has
always seemed to me that Miss Ward has had a dislike
to deal with that modern phase of the drama which has
been called the "psychological" or "problem" method;
hence, her high talents have been devoted to the
exposition of the poetic and high-class drama. Such
being the case, it was only natural that she should
become associated with the great Lyceum epoch under
Sir Henry Irving, and in such parts as Margaret of
Anjou in "Richard III," and Queen Eleanor in
"Beckett."

The name of Genevieve Ward will ever hold a high
place in the annals of English histrionic art. With her
retirement to a well-earned rest, and the close of the
Lyceum epoch, the old playgoer, and the lover of the
highest stage art can cherish pleasant memories and
tender thanks to those who have rendered aid and
expended genius on the best art of the Victorian Stage.

There can be no doubt about the influence of the
work of "The Kendals" on the histrionic art of the

Stage during the latter half of the Victorian era.
William Hunter Grimston and Margaret Robertson
(sister of the dramatist) are known in Stage annals as
"The Kendals," but Mrs. Kendal will ever live in the
memory of old playgoers as "Madge Robertson." She
captivated the hearts of all who loved genuine and
refined Stage art in her maiden lifetime, and after
marriage and alliance with Mr. Grimston a result was
achieved which placed the Kendals on a high pedestal
of fame and appreciation in association with the history
of the English Stage.

One of my earliest recollections of Mr. and Mrs.
Kendal is associated with their marriage in 1869. This
event took place in Manchester, at St. Saviour's Church,
and it was only natural that some sort of honeymoon
should be granted to the happy couple. At this time
they were members of the grand old Haymarket
Company, and I note in Edgar Pemberton's book, "The
Kendals," a statement that just as they were about to
start on their honeymoon the unwelcome news reached
them that Mr. Compton was obliged to leave Manchester for the death-bed of a relative, that "As You
Like It" had been announced, and that bride and bride-
groom must appear as Rosalind and Orlando. This
marriage had during the day become known to
Manchester citizens, and the reception afforded by a
packed house to the happy pair was one of enthusiastic
greeting and good wishes. I was present and shall
always keep in my memory the incidents of that evening,
especially when the text had reference to the loves of

Rosalind and Orlando. It was a romantic wedding day, marked by a demonstration from Manchester citizens to a man and woman they honoured for their art's sake and for their personal attractions.

Madge Robertson, in her younger days, enacted some interesting parts, but her theatrical celebrity commenced when Buckstone engaged her as a member of the Haymarket Company. It is impossible to make the present race of playgoers understand what an important result was attached to such an event in the life of an actor or actress. To belong to the old Haymarket Company was not only an honour, but it meant that talent was appreciated. Madge Robertson and Mr. Kendal were associated with the triumphs of the Haymarket until the death of John Baldwin Buckstone in 1874. During this period, Gilbert's fairy blank verse dramas were produced, and Mrs. Kendal delighted her audiences in "The Palace of Truth," "Pygmalian and Galatea," and other works of modern dramatists, such as "New Men and Old Acres," by my late friend, Tom Taylor and Dubourg. As Lilian Vavasour, in this drama, Mrs Kendal reached the highest histrionic art, and her impersonation of the part may be chronicled along with the best stage art of the Victorian era.

After the close of the Buckstone *regime* at the Haymarket, Mr. and Mrs. Kendal joined Mr. John Hare at the Court Theatre, and afterwards at the St. James's, and thus a trio of the finest stage artists was formed, which resulted in such productions as "Les Pattes de Mouche," adapted for the English Stage by

Mr. Palgrave Simpson under the title of "A Scrap of Paper." I trust there are many persons living who remember the Susan Hartley and Colonel Blake of Mrs. and Mr. Kendal. The play was an enormous success, rendered so by the genius of the Kendals. The same remark may apply to the success of "The Money Spinner," "The Squire," and "The Ironmaster," by Pinero. It is not an easy matter to define the art of the Kendals, but in considering that of Mrs. Kendal, I am certain it proves the fact that the great actor or actress is not made by academic training, but is born with that instinct which produces art of any kind, but especially that of the stage, where the varying emotions of the human heart have to be displayed through the living body, and not by canvas or marble. Mrs. Kendal, like Ellen Terry, is a born artist; hence the strong hold on the hearts of English playgoers. I think the triumphal close of the Victorian Stage art was marked by the historic event of the gifted women playing the wives, when Mr. Tree produced "The Merry Wives of Windsor," with himself as Falstaff. The event was unique in the history of English dramatic art; two great actresses of our time were seen as the two principal female personages in a Shakespearean play; one felt that the immortal dramatist was present, and that he was looking at the actual living embodiment of two of his favourite women rejoicing in their merriment and innocent mischief. Such an event is like the realisation of a great picture or a grand monumental record; and it is a fortunate thing that this work of histrionic art should have been perpetuated through the fine canvas painted by the Hon. John Collier.

The members of the trio I have alluded to in connection with the Court and St. James's Theatre's are still adorning the English Stage, and the grateful thanks of all lovers of true histrionic art will ever be affectionately tendered to "The Kendals."

It was fortunate for the comic histrionic art of the Victorian era that John Lawrence Toole should have appeared to grace the Stage of his time by his genial humour and pathos. By his wonderful comic and pathetic impersonations the art of the English Stage has been elevated, and what is called the comic element in acting has been placed on a high pinnacle of respect which in Stage annals has become monumental. It is difficult in a work like this, based on notes and recollections, to give an idea of the life-work and art of John Lawrence Toole. It may be said that to be a comic actor, a man must naturally love the light and genial side of nature; that this is the case with Toole is evident to all those who know him. In two anecdotal and gossipy volumes, entitled "Reminiscences of J. L. Toole," by Joseph Hatton, this phase of geniality of temperament and spirit of fun have been amply set forth and illustrated by many tales told by Toole himself, to which I refer my readers for amusement.

It is a curious thing, however, that in addition to the genial and comic side of his temperament, there existed, as shown in his acting, a love of the pure, the beautiful, and the pathetic in human life, Although we have often been the victims of uncontrollable laughter in such pieces as " Ici en Parle Francais," " Birthplace of Podgers," " Paul Pry," and " Robert Macaire," we cherish a delightful memory for such exquisite delineations of pathos as have been found in such character parts as Caleb Plummer, Dick Dolland, and Michael Garner.

The piece entitled " Dot" was a dramatic version of the " Cricket on the Hearth," and as a matter of course the well-known and well-beloved characters therein offered fine opportunities for the exercise of true histrionic art. It was in Caleb Plummer that Mr. Toole reached the highest art both in comedy and pathos. The image of the dear old toy-maker painting the little wooden horse rises in the mind, and a burst of laughter almost repeats itself as we hear the comic reflection after decorating the model with three or four circular blots of scarlet colour, " That's as near as I can come to nature for half-a-crown." In contrast the pathetic scenes with the dear blind Bertha stand before us, and the character as a whole illustrates the fact of the actor possessing not only quaint and genial humour, but a strong love for the refined and pathetic side of human life.

There is historic interest attached to " Uncle Dick's Darling," written by H. J. Byron, for it was in this piece that Irving played Chevenix to his dear friend's Dick Dolland. The play was a most interesting achievement, and the dream of the cheap Jack on the steps of his van was realised by fine acting. I recollect that Mary Belton was played by Miss Neilson. A thoroughly representative exposition of the highest art of acting was given in "Uncle Dick's Darling," and it is interesting to know that the greatest actor of our time, Sir Henry Irving, produced an impression on Charles Dickens in the part of Chevenix, upon which he delivered that prophetic statement of his future success, to which I have already alluded as told me by Mr. Toole himself.

Mr. Toole became, in his latter days on the stage, the lessee of the theatre in King William Street, Charing Cross. It was in this house that we who loved the artist and his art, had the opportunity of renewing our acquaintance with that wonderful repertoire upon which the reputation of Toole had been built. A notice printed from the *Sunday Times* of June 10th, 1888, sums up the *raison d'être* of the art of the king of the comic actors of the Victorian Stage. "Mr. Toole, throughout his career, has never given his audience the smallest cause of offence in regard to what he has put upon the Stage, or how he has put it on, and one cannot but rejoice at his continued success." I am sure my dear old friend, in his quiet retirement on the southern coast of this little island, must often think of the public appreciation of his art, and of the affection he has begotten in the hearts of a host of friends. " Heaven grant him many years of sunshine days!"

A feature of the art of the latter half of the Victorian era was what may be called the comic opera of Gilbert and Sullivan. Although it is not my intention to deal with the music art of the period I am writing of, it must be admitted that in those Savoy operas, much clever comic acting accompanied what became extremely popular music. The operas of " Patience," " Pinafore," " Pirates of Penzance," " Iolanthe," " The Yeomen of the Guard," and the " Gondoliers," will always stand in evidence of the genius of their authors. It is an interesting fact that Alfred Cellier and Arthur Sullivan were boys together in the choir of the Chapel Royal, St. James's. That early friendship increased in interest and value. Sir Arthur Sullivan has told me interesting anecdotes of the author of " Dorothy," and I could tell more in connection with his life in Manchester when he produced " The Sultan of Mocha," " The Tower of London," and other works. The late George Free-mantle, musical critic of the *Manchester Guardian*, in an obituary notice wrote of Cellier : " Mr. Cellier was a man of the most courtly and amiable manners. Few musicians have left so favourable a personal impression in this city. It was felt to be a loss to the town, when he removed to London, but those who had the pleasure of his acquaintance when here, are not likely to forget him.

Many notable effects have been produced by music in association with the drama. The singing of songs has often added fine and telling effect to dramatic incident and situation. Shakespeare knew the value of poetic song ; hence the many delightful effects produced by incidental music. To those who were present on that memorable evening of October 15th, 1864, when the Manchester Prince's Theatre first opened its doors, and when the curtain rose on Calvert's first Shakes-pearean revival, "The Tempest," the singing of "Where the bee sucks" by Julia St. George, as Ariel, will ever remain a precious memory. The effect of this on the audience was something extraordinary. The enthusiasm was so great, that the gifted lady had to repeat the song two or three times before the piece was allowed to proceed. This episode was a triumph for Victorian Stage art.

A similar instance of the effect of song in the drama, was T. R. Emmett's rendering of "Schneider how you vas," in his play of "Fritz." This episode became so popular, that from the moment the handsome comedian took the boy (son of the prison keeper) on his back the applause commenced, and it was some time before he was allowed to begin the song. As Emmett gracefully galloped round the stage with the boy perched aloft, and still singing, the excitement was so intense, that men shouted and women cried with delight. It was a wonderful stage incident, and as far as my knowledge goes, unique in the dramatic history of our time.

The art of our Stage during the latter portion of the reign of Queen Victoria owes much of its interest to American artistes, and the names of Mary Anderson, Genevieve Ward, Joseph Jefferson, Emmett, and Edwin Booth are enrolled in the annals of the English-speaking Stage. Many persons now living will re-member the classic beauty of Mary Anderson, and the high refinement of her art, as exhibited at the London Lyceum in 1881, in such pieces as "Ingomar,"

" Lady of Lyons," and "Pygmalian and Galatea." The reign of this delightful actress was too short on the theatrical stage, but she left an artistic impression in her own country and in England.

My knowledge of the late Joseph Jefferson and my high regard for his art, both as an actor and a painter, render my reference to him a matter of difficulty. The temptation to run into extravagant praise is very strong, whereas my object in this book is to deal with the art of the stage, as developed by gifted men and women living in the period of which I am writing. Joseph Jefferson was a born artist, and his work, whether on the easel or on the stage, was of that dreamy poetic character that it fascinated all who came under its influence. I may here include some extracts from a communication published in the *Manchester Guardian* soon after Jefferson's death.

It is not generally known that much of his spare time was devoted to the easel, or that on the occasion of his last visit to Manchester an exhibition of his works was held in the old Brazennose Club. Jefferson was a modest and rather a retiring man, and it was with some difficulty that I induced him to collect all the landscape examples he had in this country, so that Manchester artists might have a chance of seeing the standpoint from which he looked upon nature in pictorial treatment. Jefferson took nature as a basis upon which to work, but he invested it with such poetic and atmospheric wonders that his works ended in bewildering and fascinating dreams.

Jefferson's painting was, like his acting, the outcome of his own creative genius. There used to be some curious rules laid down for the exposition of the poetic drama, one being that an actor must never turn his back on his audience. A heavy blow was dealt at conventional stage art by Joseph Jefferson in his immortal "Rip Van

Winkle." It is a matter of astonishment how the true artist does the right thing on the stage, unconscious of any strain or conventional effort. I recollect discussing this matter with Jefferson, and I pointed to a curious fact in connection with his great impersonation. Many persons may still remember that one act of "Rip Van Winkle" was occupied with a "set" scene representing a high point on the Catskill Mountains; Hudson's men, deaf and dumb, occupied the scene. Jefferson had carried the little keg of "schnappes" up the mountain for the little, elfish dwarf. From the moment he set it down near the footlights not a soul spoke but Rip, and his face was never seen by the audience till he turned round, overcome by the liquor which induced the sleep of twenty years. This wonderful scene lasted, on an average, twenty minutes. On the fall of the curtain the audience demanded with enthusiasm the return of the actor who had turned his back upon them for such a length of time. This scene was a triumph of art—unconventional, and outside all academic rules of theatrical art. Jefferson did not realise that he was violating all stage canons, and simply stated that he knew of no other way of playing the scene.

Jefferson's impersonation of Rip Van Winkle may be considered one of the greatest achievements of the art of the stage. It was a beautiful thought on the part of its author; and, on the part of its delineator, was an exquisite source of delight to the thousands who witnessed the performance. An elaborate essay could be written on Jefferson's Rip; but I must rest content with saying that from the moment he rushes on the stage playing with the village children, through the period up to the beginning of the sleep of twenty years, after the wakening up, at the village of "Falling Waters," to the closing scene, we looked upon an exposition of the highest histrionic art, and such a poetic rendering of a poetic thought has never been surpassed on the stage of the nineteenth century. It is treasured in the mind with affectionate regard for the great man who enhanced the value of histrionic art on the stage of the Victorian era.

I have mentioned Emmett, and how he captivated his English audiences with the play entitled "Fritz." There were many beautiful touches of pathos in Emmett's acting, and with his untimely death, an actor was removed from the English-speaking Stage whose talents were fully appreciated, and whose kindly disposition won the hearts both of American and English playgoers.

Edwin Booth was an American actor of high repute ; but as my recollections of him are scanty, it is difficult to assign a true place for him in the art of the Stage of the period of which I am writing. I remember him coming here sometime in the early eighties, and that on leaving the London theatre where he was acting, Irving induced him to join the Lyceum Company in the production of "Othello." Irving and Booth played Othello and Iago alternately (these performances I witnessed), and it was in such characters that Booth's tragic capacity became evident, and in which he added value to the histrionic art of his time. Edwin Booth was an honour to his profession, and his name will always be held in esteem by his countrymen in America, and by his English brethren.

Although we recognise American actors and actresses as members of the English-speaking Stage, it must be admitted that the foreign artist who appears on the English Stage is entitled to some recognition, especially if the acting is of a high order and displayed in the high-class drama. The names of Fechter, Salvini, Ristori, and Bernhardt rise before the mind and rouse delightful recollections associated with the highest genius of histrionic art. It is curious and interesting to note that such a display of foreign talent should never have been seen in any other English monarch's reign, and that the reign of Victoria should have been the medium of such a presentation.

I remember Fechter's Hamlet, and the flaxen wig he used instead of the traditional black locks. I did not carry away a lasting impression of this performance, and I can only remember Salvini's savagery in connection with his treatment of Iago in "Othello." I have not forgotten that masterstroke of art when Sarah Bernhardt wrote that heart-breaking letter dictated by Armand's father, in "La Dame aux Camelia s;" but high above all this rises the genius and grandeur of that noble lady—Ristori. Such a woman and such an actress is rarely seen in Stage art; although it might be difficult to follow the exact words of a foreign text, the greatness of the play and the superb acting carried audiences along as in a torrent, and proved that humanity can be stirred and enthusiastically roused by a really great and born actor, although the tongue in which this is achieved is totally foreign to the listener.

Those who had the good fortune to see the great Ristori in "Marie Antoinette" will remember a scene in that play, which to my mind was the acme of stagecraft in the direction of realism. On September 27th, 1873, Madame Ristori gave a farewell performance of Giacometti's historical drama, at the Queen's Theatre, Manchester. At a certain point in the development of the drama one was conscious of an uncertain and mysterious sound, interpenetrating, as it were, the action on the stage. The actors became conscious of it, and seemed to pause as if to fathom its meaning. In course of time there was no mistaking its cause; the uncertain sound gradually swelled into a babel of human voices, and we knew that the rabble of Paris was on its way to Versailles. I shall never forget this piece of stage realism. The great actress allowed me to see how it was achieved; it was wonderful in its simplicity, but stupendous in result.

I had a curious experience during the performance of " Marie Antoinette," which I may relate as an instance of the power of the superlative genius of perhaps the greatest actress of our own time. I had a seat in the pit, about two rows from the stalls; on my left sat a thorough specimen of a Lancashire working woman with her daughter, a girl about fifteen years of age. These two had paid their money, not knowing that the play was in the Italian language. Shortly after the commencement of the prologue the elder woman drew a cork from a bottle, refreshed herself, and handed it to the daughter. This operation was frequently repeated. At length the woman turned to me, and said :

" I say, mester, are they gooin' to talk loike this o' neet ? "

" Yes," I said.

" Eh, dear! I wish I'd moi money back," she said.

" Perhaps you'll get interested as the play proceeds; you'll know what they are doing, although you don't understand what they are saying," I remarked.

My reply was destined to a fulfilment I little anticipated. The advent of the Parisian mob interested and astonished the simple Lancashire woman ; but when the Dauphin was dragged from the side of the unfortunate queen, human nature asserted itself. When the magnificent actress frantically threw herself across the door which shut her out for ever from her son, down dropped the obnoxious bottle with a crash ; the woman rose to her feet and shouted out, " Yo' munna tak him!" Never shall I forget the effect of this incident. A roar of Lancashire applause rose from that audience ; and I had the opportunity shortly afterwards of explaining to the great actress, through an interpreter, the precise meaning of the episode.

The world of art has been enriched by the stage work of this great actress. Italy is naturally proud of her, and the whole civilised world honours the name of Adelaide Ristori del Grillo.

There are actors and actresses still living who won renown in their art in the latter portion of the Victorian period. Charles Wyndham (now Sir Charles), J. Forbes Robertson, Boucicault, L. Brough, Alexander, Herman Vezin, Harvey, Louis Calvert, Edward Terry, Bourchier, Miss Bateman, Olga Nethersole, Mrs. Langtry, Mrs. P. Campbell, Miss Julia Neilson, Beatrice Violet and

Irene Vanbrugh, and Miss Ada Dyas. I have pleasant recollections of some of these artists, and their efforts in the portrayal of both the old and modern drama. Miss Bateman (Mrs. Crowe) achieved quite an artistic sensation in her portrayal of the parts in "Leah" and "Mary Warner;" the curse scene thrilled her audiences, and proved that she was an actress of high power.

Johnston Forbes Robertson may be said to have made his reputation in the Shakespearean drama, although he has done good work in the latest modern drama of value and interest from an artistic point of view. I well remember his first attempt at Othello at a Manchester theatre; it was a remarkable performance, and, no doubt, paved the way to "Hamlet" when he took over the Lyceum for a period. The production was rendered interesting by the effort made by Mrs. Patrick Campbell to impersonate Ophelia, and by new *business* introduced in several scenes. The last scene was rendered very effective by Hamlet dying in a sitting posture, and the curtain descending on the entrance of Vortigern and his attendants. If I remember rightly, this production ran for something like one hundred nights in 1897. It may, therefore, be classed with the Stage art work of the Victorian era.

Dion Boucicault was a person of repute, both as an author of actable plays and as an actor. Having a thorough knowledge of Irish character, he was able to produce and act in plays, in which Irish humour and pathos found an excellent medium of expression without coarseness or vulgarity. There are many persons living

who have pleasant memories of " The Colleen Bawn,"
" Arrah na Pogue," and " The Shaughraun," and the
clever acting of their author therein.   It is interesting
to note that the lady who did so much to enhance the
value of the Robertsonian drama, should afterwards
contribute so much to the success of Boucicault's Irish
drama in America.   Ada Dyas rendered the heroines
with consummate grace and art, and her representation
of Claire Ffolliott has taken its place in the art of the
Victorian Stage.   Miss Dyas has played many beautiful
parts with distinction.   She inherited histrionic faculty
from both parents, who were well known on the stage
of the middle period of the Victorian era.   Her American
triumphs are matters of history, and her last appearance
on the English Stage was to assist her old friend, Sir
Henry Irving, in his revival of "King Lear."   My dear
old friend, with whom I played in the Lancashire
celebration of the tercentenary of Shakespeare, now
rests on her well-earned laurels in a beautiful rural
cot in a pastoral southern county.

Although it is a melancholy matter of duty, I must
say a few words upon the work of those who have left
the histrionic Stage for "the unknown country, from
whose bourne no traveller returns."

Of those artists who departed this life in the Victorian
period, the names of Coleman, Vandenhoff, W. Mon-
gomery, Swinbourne, G. V. Brooke, Charles Matthews,
Wilson Barrett and H. J. Montague must be recorded,
as representing the highest phase of the drama, prior
to that which has been placed before the theatre-going

public for some years past. I remember Wilson Barrett trying "Hamlet" at the Princesses' Theatre, but the experiment did not produce a lasting impression on the mind. In the higher phase of melo-drama he was, however, supreme. Such pieces as "The Silver King," "The Sign of the Cross," and "Claudian" afforded Barrett opportunities of exercising his histrionic gifts to the pleasure and delight of his audiences. He may be justly classed with those who have contributed to the art of the Victorian Stage.

I had personal acquaintance with Coleman, W. Montgomery, and Swinburne, but their contribution to the art of the period I am writing of was not of much importance in the history and development of that school of art which consigned conventional and academic acting to the shadows of the past. G. V. Brooke was of the same school of acting, his life has been written by W. J. Lawrence. I have pleasant memories of the art of Adelaide Lee Neilson, and of H. J. Montague and Herman Vezin, also I remember the humour and comedy acting of Charles Matthews. These artists took honourable places in the histrionic period of which I am writing, and of which my notes and recollections are nearly exhausted.

In concluding my remarks on the modern drama, which was rendered on the stage in the last years of the Victorian era, I cannot find much to say in favour of that which is associated with the authorship of Ibsen; but I must record the fact, that two clever women did their best to make it understood and appreciated. The names of Elizabeth Robins and Janet Achurch must be regarded with respect. These actresses had a difficult task to perform, and their efforts are worthy of all praise.

It is not within the scope of this work to review the works of modern dramatists apart from their stage representations by the managers and actors of the Victorian period. It is, however, desirable that in addition to the dramatic authors already alluded to, the names of others should be recorded who have contributed to the dramatic literature of the Victorian Stage. It is curious that many of these authors, and their works, are not known to the present race of playgoers. We never see the plays of Bulwer Lytton (Lord Lytton), but there are persons living who will remember the pleasure they got out of "The Lady of Lyons," "Money," and other plays by this author, and in which every actor or actress of position played. Wilkie Collins was a name which represented high-class, modern drama, and his "Woman in White" is enrolled with the best drama which found stage expression in the latter half of the Victorian era.

Some of the latest writers of the last reign have achieved reputation and provided a medium for histrionic display by players like Martin Harvey, Lewis Waller, George Alexander, Julia Neilson, Bruce, Beerbohm Tree, Louis Calvert, Lionel Brough, Mrs. Patrick Campbell and Olga Nethersole.

Several of these writers, it must be confessed, have drifted into that phase of the drama which has been called "problem" work, and for which I have no sympathy or regard. I must, however, express high regard for some of the work done for the stage by Henry Arthur Jones, Pinero, Carr, Barrie, Phillips, Hermann Merivale, Conan Doyle, Sir Gilbert Parker, Louis N. Parker, Andrew Halliday, E. Abbott Parry (Judge Parry), and the late Lord Tennyson.

It is a source of high satisfaction to all lovers of the best art of the Stage, that amidst what may be called the triviality of present Stage work, there is at least one modern author who can provide high-class drama, and for almost the only actor, who dared to persist in the representation of the Shakespearean and historic drama. Phillips and Tree, are now supreme, and represent the highest art of the present time. *Floreat!*

My last words are written whilst Ellen Terry is celebrating her stage jubilee; but although I have alluded to the work and art of this charming and highly gifted actress, I cannot close these notes and recollections without adding my tribute of respect and admiration for one who has made such a mark on the Stage art of the period of which I have written. Her impersonaation of Shakespearean heroines is a delightful memory; and when creating a part of a modern playwright, her genius has shown us wonderful results. English-speaking people may feel proud of Ellen Terry and the work she has done for the refinement and beauty of the histrionic art of the Stage in the Victorian era.

CHAPTER IX.

THEATRE BUILDING.

ALTHOUGH I have hitherto treated of the art displayed on the Victorian Stage, it seems desirable that a word should be said on the buildings in which the drama has been displayed in this country. It is a proof of the growth of the modern love of dramatic representation that theatres have increased in number and variety, especially during the latter half of the Victorian era. In the building and decoration of these homes of the drama the wishes and desires of the proprietors were alone consulted, but in many cases the comfort and convenience of the audience have been amply provided for. From an architectural point of view, some of the façades of recent theatres are good and well designed, and the internal decoration in some cases is of a high order of merit. There is one feature in connection with the planning of the modern theatre which has been forced upon our attention by disaster and the loss of human life. I allude to the means of escape in case of fire panic. Whilst a good sight of the stage, good acoustic properties and a well-complete appointed stage are essentials to theatre building, the prevention of fire and the ready means of exit are vital points for consideration in the planning of a theatre.

This matter of a safe theatre in case of fire has caused me serious and anxious thought, and in my professional work in the planning and erection of theatres, I have laid down certain conditions, the realisation of which I will always insist upon. I have considered it desirable to place these conditions on record, and by the kindness of the British Fire Prevention Committee I am enabled to quote my paper on "Theatre Exits," written after the planning of the "Safety Theatre," which was suggested and thought out by my friend, Sir Henry Irving.

In the year 1869 my attention was drawn to theatre architecture. I was consulted by the proprietors of the Prince's Theatre, in the city of Manchester, with a view to various alterations and improvements in the little house, which afterwards became famous for the production of the Shakspearean drama. It was during the progress of this work that I became conscious of the shortcomings of English theatre planning in the matter of safety to the public in case of panic. Like many other theatres, the Manchester Prince's was built in between other properties, with only means of exit on the street facade for the public; the stage and its adjuncts being approached from a back street. Without forming, at the time I am speaking of, any definite ideas as to what should be done to avoid these unsatisfactory conditions, I was nevertheless convinced, that in the event of fire panic, the consequences would be fatal and disastrous.

Theatre architecture, however, still continued on these unsatisfactory lines, and it was not until the year 1887, when the awful disaster occurred at the Exeter Theatre, that the public mind became thoroughly aroused to the inadequacy of English theatre planning and construction. It was after this tragedy at Exeter, that our greatest actor-manager, Sir Henry Irving, consulted me on the possibility of designing a theatre which should possess all the elements of safety to the frequenters of the play-house.

During my frequent work in connection with theatre architecture, I had gradually formulated plans of reform; I was therefore prepared to enter heartily into the solution of the problem which Sir Henry Irving submitted for my serious consideration. I will explain the conclusions arrived at after careful thought and much discussion, and allude to the practical working out of those conclusions in theatres actually erected on the lines of the scheme which we jointly formulated.

At this point, I may say that I believe the time has arrived when theatre planning must be subjected to municipal or State control, and I cannot understand how any argument can be advanced against such a proposition. It is my firm conviction that every detail of arrangement and construction should be distinctly fixed, and that it should be impossible for any theatre to be erected unless in strict conformity with rules and regulations of some recognised authority for the safety of theatrical or other audiences using public buildings. The time has arrived for a complete revolution in theatre planning, and that adequate provision in the way of exit must be insisted upon in all buildings where the public are to be gathered in any numbers. We must get rid of prejudice in favour of the old system ; and as Hamlet says, "reform it altogether."

It is not my purpose in this paper to consider fire-proof construction or fire extinction. These matters are of secondary importance when the safety of a public audience has to be secured. What is the meaning of the word safety as applied to an audience, or to a mass of people in a public building? There can only be one opinion on this point. It means the provision of *instant* and *direct escape* from a building when attacked by fire; in other words, clear and adequate planning. Mr. Sachs, in his excellent paper on the dreadful Paris Charity Bazaar fire, has used these words : "Personally, I hold that for a theatre or music hall, *clear planning is of greater importance to the audience* than clever forms of construction or the employment of materials having considerable power of fire resistance." These words embody a great truth, and they represent exactly the method and practice I have endeavoured to maintain since the disaster at Exeter in 1887.

The provision of *instant and direct escape*, or in other words clear planning, is the subject on which I propose to offer a few remarks in this paper.

The whole question of safe theatre planning may

be described in one sentence, namely, *ample and direct means of exit*. After this condition has been realised, fire-proof construction and fire extinction appliances may be considered. In other words, after the destruction of human life has been reduced to a minimum or rendered impossible, the destruction of property may receive that consideration calculated to reduce monetary loss.

It will be at once admitted, that in order to secure complete and perfect exit from a theatre, the building must stand on an isolated site; in other words, that it must be surrounded either by open spaces, streets or roads. I shall be told that this is (especially in the metropolis) a condition impossible of realisation. My reply to such an allegation is, that possible or impossible of realisation, I should so order legislation, that no theatre of the future should be allowed to be erected unless this initial condition of isolation be carried out in some form. At this point it is interesting to record the fact, that this vital condition has become law with the Corporation of the City of Manchester, and that no new theatre in the future will be permitted without this principle of isolation, to give it a *raison d'être*.

I need hardly point out, that a theatre situated on an isolated site affords the architect every opportunity of securing ample and direct exit. Assuming that it is impossible to find or secure in our large English cities such fine open sites such as we see in many continental capitals, and, moreover, if such sites could be found, that the cost involved would be so immense that no theatre could be realised and maintained unless by municipal or

State aid, let us consider what compromise may be arrived at by which isolation of our theatres may be secured.

If fine open sites cannot be found, or are impossible to the builder of a theatre in an English city, it is clear that they must in some manner be *created* or made. It is not necessary for the purpose of secure and certain exit that a building should be architecturally beautiful or imposing on all its façades (as is often the case abroad) but what I maintain is, that it should have roadways or streets of some description on *all sides.* These will probably exist at the front and back, but they must be *made* to exist at the sides. Now how is this to be done? Either by securing land enough or reducing the area of the building. It is only necessary that these roadways or streets should be wide enough to allow persons, escaping from the theatre, access to the main thoroughfares. This expedient of creating streets was resorted to in the case of the Palace Theatre of Varieties, erected within the last few years in Manchester. On three sides of the site streets existed, and by decreasing the width of the building a narrow street or roadway was created, and by which safe planning and direct exit were achieved. I introduce this recent instance because it illustrates the point I wish to maintain, namely, that it *is* possible to secure the great principle of isolation, and consequently, direct exit on all sides of the building.

Having secured an isolated site for a theatre, I will point out what I consider essential in the proper planning of entrances and exits. The primary condition is, that every part of the house (including the orchestra) shall have at least one entrance and one exit; this will be equivalent to two exits to each part in case of panic. As a matter of course, those persons behind the curtain must have equal provision for escape, but it will suffice to deal with the auditorium, or that portion occupied by hundreds, sometimes by thousands, of human beings. Secondly, where it is necessary for those exits to be provided with steps or staircases they must be constructed with straight steps throughout; and if more than one flight is required they must be built into a centre stone wall. There must on no account be any winding or circular steps, and the maximum rise must be six inches. Furthermore, there must not be any obstruction or pay boxes on these stairs and exits; the whole must be absolutely clear, and the only openings therein must be the one at the street, and the other at the top leading into the auditorium. Both doors in these openings must swing *outwards* and be provided with exit locks, which act instantly by pressure, and which are now brought to a high state of mechanical excellence.

Another condition to be insisted upon with regard to exits is, that they must be on *opposite* sides of the auditorium, and towards the front of the building. When a fire breaks out in a theatre it is on the stage. Self-preservation is the first law of nature. Therefore, panic-stricken persons fly *from* the scene of danger and not towards it. The minimum width of auditorium staircases and exits must be fixed at five feet, with a wall handrail on each side. If staircases are six feet wide or more, they must be divided by a centre handrail. If the staircase is a single flight, there must be no landing of any description; these level or broken spaces in a straight staircase are a source of danger to a panic-stricken audience. In these days of advanced fireproof construction, it is not necessary for me to say that all exit staircases should be built of stone or concrete. I maintain, however, that material is of no consequence as regards the safety of an escaping audience. If they are planned and arranged in the manner I have pointed out, an audience would be free of the building long before any fire could reach the means of escape.

Although the object of this paper is to treat only with safe planning and sure escape from a burning theatre, I may be allowed to record that contingencies have arisen which have prevented an audience, or portion of an audience, from reaching the means of exit. It may be a matter of surprise to many persons to learn that the loss of life in a fire panic in a theatre or buildings used for public audiences is not owing to fire (I do not include such flimsy and quick-burning buildings as the one used for the Paris Charity Bazaar) or to actual contact with flame, but to asphyxiation or suffocation by inhaling the poisonous gases given off during conflagration. At Exeter, the poor creatures sitting in the gallery never left their seats, for when the cloud of poison burst from the stage it instantly ascended, enveloped them, and left them sitting as at the play, but so many rows of ghastly corpses, instead of the merry human beings who had shortly before entered that theatre full of health and life.

This awful episode at Exeter has taught us two lessons ; the first is that no seat should be placed higher than the proscenium opening. It is clear that to realise this condition, a third tier is quite impossible, and in fact should never be allowed in modern theatre planning. In order to place the second or top tier as near the street level as possible, the pit must be sunk below the level of the surrounding streets. This arrangement has been carried out in the New Exeter Theatre, and in the great Theatre of Varieties and the Comedy Theatre in Manchester. In these theatres, the dress circle is level, or nearly level, with the streets, and the highest point at which any portion of the audience is placed is twenty-three feet from the street. It may appear, on first consideration of this arrangement; that to sink so large a portion of the audience is open to objection; but experience has proved that rather than objectionable it is advantageous. The descent to the pit is achieved by inclines and steps, and an audience accepts the arrangement without demur. Moreover, in case of a stampede from panic, the chances of disaster to life are less to an ascending audience than to a descending one. I do not advocate the sinking of a *whole theatre* below the street level, as I believe is the case at one London theatre, because the asphyxiating fumes can only find a way out by the staircases, which would act as draft tunnels, and the ascending audiences would run the risk of

suffocation during their efforts to escape to the street
levels.

The second lesson we learn from the Exeter disaster
is, that means should be provided for the instant isolation
of the stage from the auditorium. This can now be done
with ease and certainty. We have now fireproof curtains
which can be dropped and which seal up the proscenium
opening in something like ten seconds. It may here
be remarked that no opening except the proscenium
one should be allowed in the wall which divides the
stage from the auditorium; the means of communication
between these two parts of the building must be
external, and the same arrangement applies to the
orchestra. The proscenium opening being closed in
and the fire confined to the stage, with the open
louvred funnel in the centre of the roof acting as a
draft shaft, it is not necessary to tell anyone acquainted
with the action of fire what the result would be. In
the first place the audience is safe from suffocation, and
secondly the fire on the stage will soon be under
control, and great loss of property will in consequence
be avoided.

As this paper is devoted to a consideration of the
theatre exits, I must not lengthen it by reference to
other matters of interest to the architect of buildings
devoted to the uses of the theatre. I must, however,
point out to theatre managers that it is absolutely
essential that all gangways, passages, or corridors communicating with or leading to exits should be kept open
and free of extra chairs, or furniture objects, in the way

of those who, panic-stricken, fly to the doors at the top of the exit staircases or passages. In any legislation connected with the building and maintenance of public buildings, neglect of this matter should be made a criminal offence.

In conclusion, I venture to think that if the safe planning I have advocated be insisted upon by properly constituted authority, the disasters of the past would be avoided, and rendered impossible in the future.

I append to this some notes written by Mr. Edwin O. Sachs, Chairman of the Executive of the British Fire Prevention Committee, and author of a treatise entitled "The Housing of the Drama" and "Modern Opera Houses and Theatres."

The great theatre fires of 1881 and 1887 turned the thoughts of architects and public officials to a serious consideration of fire and panic prevention in theatres; but Sir Henry Irving was the only English manager who gave emphatic expression to his thoughts on the subject by a set of plans prepared in consultation with his architect, Mr. Alfred Darbyshire, of Manchester. The plans were published in the columns of the *Daily Telegraph* in October, 1887, accompanied by interesting notes.

The problem for solution in Sir Henry Irving's scheme involved the working out of certain absolute conditions, which may be thus briefly enumerated :—

The *initial* condition is that the theatres of the future must stand completely isolated from other property, and if suitable sites cannot be obtained, then it is hoped that the controlling authorities will forbid their erection. It will easily be seen that this condition of isolation will enable an audience to escape from all sides of the auditorium.

The *second* condition of importance is that the stage shall be instantly isolated from the auditorium by the closing of the proscenium opening. All fires originate on the stage, therefore the asphyxiating fumes must be confined to the place of their origin.

The *third* condition is that the highest point accessible by an audience shall be as near to the streets as possible, and no seat shall be higher than the proscenium opening ; this is a necessary condition in case the means of stage isolation should fail.

The *fourth* condition is that every part of the house should be provided with two exits, communicating separately and direct with the streets, and having no openings in them except at the top and bottom.

The *fifth* condition is that the stage must have a fire-proof roof, provided with a large smoke shaft filled with glazed louvres. In case of fire (the proscenium opening being closed) both flame and smoke will at once make for the shaft. The firemen may then enter the stage and extinguish the fire.

The *sixth* condition is an important one. Every space upon which the human foot is planted in the auditorium and escape staircases should be absolutely fire resisting.

The foregoing conditions apply also to those portions of the theatre devoted to the artistes and those employed behind the curtain.

These conditions will constitute a safe theatre, and are realised in the plans of Sir Henry Irving's scheme.[1]

[1] This "Safety" plan was adopted by Mr. Darbyshire at the New Exeter Theatre Royal, and the Palace Theatre of Varieties, Manchester.

APPENDIX.

CALVERT MEMORIAL PERFORMANCE.

The Committee appointed to organise a Dramatic Enter-
tainment in recognition of the services rendered by the late
MR. CHARLES CALVERT to Dramatic Art, and in aid of his
Family, have to announce the generous compliance of MISS
HELEN FAUCIT (MRS. THEODORE MARTIN) with their
invitation to aid their efforts by again appearing on the stage
for one night, in her favourite character of Rosalind in
Shakespeare's Comedy of

"AS YOU LIKE IT,"

which will be performed at the Theatre Royal, Manchester, on
Wednesday, the first of October, and on Thursday, the second
of October. Miss Wallis has at the solicitation of the Committee,
generously undertaken to play the same part on the repetition
of the Comedy. The following will be the cast:—

Duke (living in exile)	B. Lee, Esq.
First Lord	J. D. Watson, S.P.W.C.
Second Lord	J. Charlton, Esq.
Amiens (with songs) . .	G. du Maurier, Esq. (" Punch ")
Jaques	A. Darbyshire, F.I.B.A.
Duke Frederick (usurping) . .	Henry J. Jennings, Esq. (Birmingham Mail)
Le Beau . , . . .	L. Alma Tadema R.A.
Charles (the Wrestler)	Edmund Yates, Esq.
Oliver	A. H. Marsh, Esq.
Jaques de Bois	Ben Brierley, Esq.
Orlando	Hon. Lewis Wingfield
Adam } Touchstone }	Tom Taylor, Esq.

Corin .   .   .   .   Lindley Sambourne Esq., (" Punch")

Sylvius.   .   .   Arthur Poole, Esq. (Manchester Histrionic Society)

William   .   .   .   .   F. C. Burnand, Esq. (" Punch ")

Rosalind (first night) , ... Miss Helen Faucit.

    ditto   (second night)   .   .   .   .   .   Miss Wallis.

Celia .   .   .   Miss Kate Pattison (By kind permission of Messrs. Kendal and Hare)

Phebe .   .   .   .   . Miss Emma Toms (Theatre Royal)

Audrey   .   .   .   . Mrs. Edward Saker.

Lords attending on Usurping Duke and Banished Duke.

By Gentlemen Amateurs.

(Members of Dramatic Societies of Manchester)

First Forester   .   .   .   .   .   . Edwin Waugh, Esq.

Ladies of the Court and Shepherdesses   .   .   . By Lady Amateurs of Manchester.

The Chorus, composed of the Royal and Prince's Choirs, under the direction of Mr. Yarwood, Composer of Ballad music, etc.

The Orchestra will be conducted by Dr. Arthur Sullivan (his health permitting)

The Memorial Programme designed by H. Stacey Marks, R.A.

The Address will be written by Mr. H. M. Acton.

The Theatre is placed at the disposal of the Committee by the kindness of the Lessees, Messrs. Duffield and Lawton.

Mr. J. Crook, of the Theatre Royal, will kindly rehearse and superintend the music. Mr. John Byrnes and his Staff will render their services; and Mr. John Watmough will work the Gas, Lime, and Electric Lights.

The production will be under the superintendence of Mr. E. Edmonds, who will kindly assist the Committee in mounting the Piece in a complete and efficient manner.

———

This circular including the names of the Committee was arranged in advertising form in the Manchester newspapers.

THE PRINCE'S THEATRE, MANCHESTER.

The Theatre opened on October 15th, 1864, with Calvert's first Revival of the "Tempest," and which inaugurated a decade of Shakespearean production now historic in the Annals of the Art of the Victorian Stage.
The following was the Cast :

Prospero	Mr. Charles Calvert
Antonio	Mr. Philip Day.
Alonso	Mr. Wainwright.
Sebastian.	Mr. Holman.
Ferdinand	Mr. H. S. Haynes.
Gonzalo	Mr. Bertram.
Adrian	Mr. Barrier.
Francisco	Mr. Russell.
Caliban	Mr. J. L Cathcart.
Trinculo	Mr. Hudspeth.
Stephano.	Mr. Edwin Dixon.
Boatswain	Mr. Markham.
Miranda	Mrs. Charles Calvert.
Ariel	Miss Julia St. George.

With the exception of Purcell's and Dr. Arne's songs, the music was composed by Mr. A. S. Sullivan.

In the Burlesque which followed, Mr. Frederick Maccabe played a part ; he with Mr. Philip Day played the brothers in their celebrated exposure of the Devenport tricks under the guidance of Henry Irving in the part of Dr. Ferguson.

The players in "The Tempest" stood loyally to their manager, and contributed to the great success of the artistic productions at the Prince's Theatre under the management of Charles Alexander Calvert.

THE COURTNEIDGE REVIVALS.

Although the Courtneidge revivals came after the death of Queen Victoria and in the first two years of the Edwardian Era, they grew out of the methods of the art of the Victorian stage ; aud cannot be separated therefrom.

The Cast of these two remarkable Revivals by Mr. Robert Courtneidge of "A Midsummer Night's Dream" and "As You Like It," is interesting as a list of actors and actresses whose methods have produced what is often called the New School of acting, or the latest phase of Victorian histrionic art. Although the methods of this New School cannot well be applied to the poetry and grandeur of Tragedy they materially help to develope the beauties and delights which emanate from Comedy ; and I have no hesitation in saying, that this style of acting combined wiih the exquisite beauty of production have rendered the two Comedies immortal in the history of stage art.

"A MIDSUMMER NIGHT'S DREAM."

Produced at the Prince's Theatre, Manchester, by Mr. Robert Courtneidge, September 7th, 1901.

CAST :

Theseus	Mr. Henry Vibart.
Egeus	Mr. E. Storey Gofton.
Lysander . . .	Mr. Conway Tearle.
Demetrius . . .	Mr. Gerald Kay Souper.
Philostrate . . .	Mr. Alfred W. Taylor.
Quince	Mr. E. Lyall-Swete.
Snug	Mr. E. W. Royce.

Bottom	Mr. W. H. Denny.
Flute	Mr. Stanley Lathbury.
Snout	Mr. W. H. Kitts.
Starveling . . .	Mr. O. B. Clarence.
Hippolyta . . .	Miss May Yelman.
Hermia	Miss Dora Barton.
Helena	Miss Ada Ferrar.
Oberon	Miss Dora Rignold.
Titania	Miss Nora Kerin.
Puck	Miss Rosie Begarnie.
Fairy	Miss Laurie Collier.
Peasblossom . . .	Miss Cicely Courtneidge.
Cobweb	Miss Francis Tritschler.
Moth	Miss Marie Dean.
Mustardseed . . .	Miss Doris Payne.

"AS YOU LIKE IT."

Produced at the Prince's Theatre, Manchester, September 16th, 1902, with the following cast:—

Duke	Mr. Edwin Holloway.
Frederick . . .	Mr. Charles Rivington.
Amiens	Mr. John Doran.
Jaques	Mr. Holbrook Blimm.
First Lord . . .	Mr. T. W. Rawson.
Le Beau	Mr. Cecil Brooking.
Charles	Mr. A. T. Hendon.
Oliver	Mr Gerald Kay Souper.
Jaques	Mr. G. Hilliard.
Orlando	Mr. Gerald Lawrence.
Adam	Mr. O. B. Clarence.
Dennis	Mr. N. H. Worrall.

Touchstone	Mr. Courtice Pounds.
Sir Oliver Martext . .	Mr. Norman Aveling.
Corin	Mr. E. Edmonds.
Sylvius	Mr. Milton Rosmer.
William.	Mr. Stanley Lathbury.
Pages	Masters Gray and Wrigley.
Rosalind	Miss Nora Kerin.
Celia	Miss Jenny Buckle.
Phœbe	Miss Marie Rignold.
Audrey.	Miss Clare Greet.